# MEMOIR OF THE EARLY LIFE OF
# WILLIAM COWPER

# WILLIAM COWPER

Carmine nobilem

# Memoir of the Early Life of William Cowper

Written by himself

## WILLIAM COWPER

Preface by Richard Edwards

An Appendix of some of Cowper's Religious Letters

Interesting Documents illustrative of the Memoir
by Samuel  Miller and William Hayley

CURIOSMITH

Minneapolis

Published by Curiosmith.
Minneapolis, Minnesota.
Internet: curiosmith.com.

Previously published by RICHARD EDWARDS, 1816.

Footnotes from the source text are labeled as "Original footnote."

Scripture quotations designated (NIV) are from the Holy Bible, NEW
INTERNATIONAL VERSION®. Copyright © 1973, 1978, 1984 by
Biblica, Inc. All rights reserved worldwide. Used by permission.

The "Guide to the Contents" was added to this edition by the publisher.

The frontispiece portrait is by William Blake after George Romney.

Supplementary content, book layout and cover design:
Copyright © 2017 Charles J. Doe.

ISBN  9781946145192

# GUIDE TO THE CONTENTS
———∘◦⚬◦∘———

# The Publisher's Preface[1]

In every thing which connects itself with the name of COWPER, the Public has long been disposed to feel a lively interest. That name is justly venerated by all who know how to appreciate the claims of genius; and is peculiarly dear to the friends of Christianity, because he to whom it belonged was the able and successful advocate of a cause which they supremely love, and in him they recognize with exultation "The POET OF THE NEW TESTAMENT."

The history of COWPER, as a man of letters and a poet, has been presented to the world by his accomplished friend, MR. HAYLEY, in a manner which has obtained general commendation. It must, however, be allowed, that a fuller illustration of COWPER's *religious* life, than any which has yet appeared, is a *desideratum*[2] in biography. That *desideratum* this

---

1 The original Publisher's Preface, by Richard Edwards, 1816.
2 Desideratum—That which is desired; that which is not possessed, but which is desirable.

little volume will, at least in part, supply; and to those who feel the peculiar charm and excellence of COWPER's style and manner, it will be the more acceptable, because the Memoir which it contains was written by his own hand.

This Document, now for the first time printed, affords internal evidence that it is the genuine composition of the elegant Poet, whose early life, and varied exercises of mind, it so affectingly describes. MR. HAYLEY, too, has stamped it as authentic, by alluding to it as "a sketch which he (COWPER) once formed himself of passages in his early life."[1] As to the reasons which have hitherto occasioned its suppression, the Publisher does not deem it necessary for him to state his conjectures; and much less does he intend to discuss the validity of those reasons, in reference to the period which immediately succeeded to the Poet's death. The motives of that delicate abstinence from all minute details, on the subject of COWPER's derangement, which MR. HAYLEY then thought it proper to observe, were, doubtless, of the most honorable kind. But the lapse of years, and consequent change of circumstances, may render that advisable at one time, which was once objectionable. Particulars, which could not be conveniently introduced in a general work, like that of MR. HAYLEY, may yet be very interesting to a numerous class of readers, and properly presented

1 Hayley's *Life of Cowper*, vol. 1, p. 94, 8vo, Ed. 1812.

to them in a separate form. And above all, in such a case as this, there may be considerations of moral utility, in favor of a circumstantial publication, which ought to overrule, and supersede all considerations of mere personal delicacy. The Publisher is satisfied that these are principles which apply to COWPER's Memoir of Himself, and which fully justify him in rescuing it from privacy, and in giving to it the facilities of universal circulation. He is of opinion, that if the excellent Poet himself could be consulted, he would direct, not its suppression, but its publication; under the persuasion, that its details will be the most efficient means of correcting certain false notions, unfriendly to spiritual religion, which some have thought themselves sanctioned in entertaining, by the vague and indistinct accounts which were previously before the world. Statements have been made, which contained perhaps *the truth*, but not that *whole truth*, the knowledge of which was essential to a right judgment on the case. The effect of such partial statements, an effect probably not always designed by those who made them, has been an impression on the minds of many, that COWPER's derangement had, from its very commencement, assumed the form and character of religious despondency. It was a debt of justice to religion, to evince that such an impression is contrary to truth; and that the oft-refuted calumny, which pretends that Piety has a direct tendency to produce insanity, can derive no support from the facts of this interesting case. The judicious and impartial reader of the following Memoir, will, it is believed, be conducted to an opposite opinion; especially when he examines, in connection with it, the admirable Letters of the Poet to LADY HESKETH and to MRS. COWPER, which, as eminently calculated to illustrate the nature and effects of his religious views and feelings, are annexed to the Memoir, by the obliging permission of the Proprietors, and form No. I of the *Appendix*.

The mental malady of COWPER evidently had its *origin* in an excessive sensibility, to which he was by nature subject, and which amounted from the first to a *constitutional tendency* towards derangement. This morbid tendency, perhaps, no combination of circumstances, however favorable, no system of education, however prudent, could have *wholly* counteracted; but it was certainly confirmed and increased by the circumstances in which he was actually placed, and by the habits of his early life. The loss of maternal tenderness and vigilance, which it was his lot to sustain in his very childhood—his education in large schools, where his feelings were kept in perpetual excitement by the irritations of that vexatious tyranny which was exercised toward him by some of the elder pupils—his destination to a profession uncongenial to his taste and disposition—and, finally, the terrors which his vivid imagination associated with an examination at the bar of the House of Lords, as to his fitness for the office to which he had been nominated—these were circumstances which fatally contributed to the ultimate disturbance of his faculties, and to all the painful events of his subsequent life. Religion was so far from causing that disturbance in the first instance, either directly or indirectly, that, even in his earliest depressions, it was the only source from which any feelings of a counteractive or consolatory nature were derived. The reader will find, that a sentiment recorded in Holy Scripture, "I will not be afraid of what man can do unto me,"[1] was the first which refreshed and relieved his tender spirit, when smarting under the lash of youthful tyranny.—At another period, namely, during his residence in the Temple, it will be seen, that his dejection was never so much alleviated as while reading the pious poems of HERBERT; poems however, which he was strangely advised to lay aside, as likely to nourish his disorder. Thus obstinate prejudice, and irreligious theory, were set up in opposition to fact and experience! So *unphilosophical*, as well as unchristian, is the wisdom of this world, when it intermeddles with the things of GOD.—In what appears to have been the first decided fit or paroxysm of his disease, prayer to GOD was the expedient, which, though it did not effect a cure, afforded, however, what nothing

1 Psalm 56:4.

else did, an important temporary solace to his spirits. Who can help lamenting that, at this critical season, he was not favored with the friendship and counsel of some person of established judgment and piety, who might have explained to him that voice of GOD, which he so indistinctly knew, and guided his feet into the way of peace. Then, instead of abandoning the practice of devotion, from which he had begun to derive substantial consolation, and of falling, first into habits of sinful dissipation, and afterwards into the gloom of despondency, he might possibly have found not only rest for his soul, but a measure of permanent relief even from his constitutional malady.—It will also be observed, that those attempts on his own life, made at a still later period, the history of which will be read with awful interest, so far from being prompted by religious principles of any kind, were in truth the effects of mental disorder, excited and aggravated by occurrences altogether secular in their nature. The circumstance of his imagining that a letter, which he accidentally read in the newspapers, was a satire on himself, and *intended* to hasten the execution of his suicidal projects, evinces that his mind at that time, not merely, as he says, "began to be disordered," but was far advanced in its progress towards complete insanity. And all these events took place long before he had adopted those views of religion, to which some have attributed the whole mischief. It will generally be found, that, when we hear it alleged that *much religion* has made men mad, there is as little of reason or of truth in the allegation, as in the similar accusation which was once brought against *much learning*, in the well-known case of the Apostle PAUL. It would be much more consistent with probability, to affirm in reference to COWPER, that his early terrors and troubles might have been materially diminished, and his comfort through life essentially promoted, if he had been taught in his youthful years the genuine doctrines of Christianity, and had made that personal application of them to the concerns of his own soul, which leads, by the blessing of GOD, to the experience of their power to relieve the conscience, and to purify the heart.

To such an experience of the consolatory and sanctifying influences of the Gospel he did subsequently attain. It is true, that Repentance towards GOD prepared the way for Faith in our Lord JESUS CHRIST; and that the conviction of sin, which produced in him the repentance, were of the most painful kind. And it must also be conceded, that with these convictions, however scriptural in their nature, and as to their *substance* the genuine result of divine agency, by which his understanding was enlightened, and his conscience effectually aroused from its slumbers, certain terrors were associated which partook of the character of mental disease. Such was the despair of obtaining present pardon, or final salvation, which for a season drank up his spirits. Nor will any man of candor be surprised, that when, for the first time, a deep concern about the interests of eternity took full possession of a mind, already the prey of morbid sensibility, and connected with a bodily frame which had been weakened and disordered by recent occurrences, the immediate result should have been the exacerbation, rather than the mitigation, of those symptoms which betokened the previous existence of derangement. How much of his subsequent agony of mind was the direct and unavoidable result of the operation of divine truth and grace—the work of the Holy Spirit who was bringing him to Christ—and how much of it was the effect of that physical disease, which his religious convictions *found*, but did not *create,* (though they might for season indirectly increase them) no human sagacity can accurately determine. Nor is the determination of that matter at all necessary for the vindication of scriptural Piety. It is sufficient to state, that, as far as the smart of COWPER's wounded spirit was occasioned by any cause of a religious nature, he was wounded only in order that he might be the more effectually healed. He happily found in DR. COTTON a physician who knew how to "minister to a mind diseased," and who could apply to the relief of his suffering patient the resources of religion as well as of medical science. And at length, by the special blessing of GOD on the perusal of his own word, the cloud of despondency was removed, and the dawning fight was matured into perfect day.

As the subject of these remarks, is one of more than ordinary importance, the Publisher has inserted, in No. II of the *Appendix*, some interesting observations, which originally appeared in a valuable periodical work, and which, he trusts, will be the more acceptable, because they are connected with a brief sketch of the Poet's history, from the period at which the Memoir concludes to the time of his death. This volume will thus present, at one view, and in a small compass, a complete account of the *religious* life of COWPER, such as cannot elsewhere be found.

No. III of the *Appendix* consists of *Observations on the Sin of Suicide*. They are chiefly extracted from the Sermons of an eminent American Divine, which have not before been reprinted in this country. The subject is introduced into this volume, from a desire to furnish to every reader a ready and ample confutation of certain false reasonings, to which allusions are made in some parts of the Memoir. The fact, that COWPER made attempts on his own life, was before known to many. The details, now published, will tend, it is hoped, to increase in every reader, that natural horror, with which such attempts are usually contemplated. And the extracts inserted in the *Appendix* will show, that not only the common feelings of our nature, but all the authority which sound argument can claim over the understanding, and all the solemnity which attends a well-founded appeal to the conscience, are directly opposed, on this point, to the destructive suggestions of melancholy, and to the sophisms of infidel philosophy. Suicide, unless when committed under the influence of such a total insanity, as must altogether destroy responsibility, is undoubtedly, to use the energetic language of COWPER, "a passage to the bottomless pit." This abstract principle there can be no hesitation in maintaining; while, at the same time, we must often leave the particular application of it to Him, whose infinite wisdom alone is competent to define the boundaries between such a partial derangement, as does not destroy accountability, and such a complete and perfect suspension of the faculties, as puts the individual out of the pale of moral government. The Judge of all the earth will do right.

The Publisher thinks it right to state that he is not responsible for the correctness of every sentiment found in the Memoir. As to the divine directions, with which COWPER believed himself to be favored in dreams, or by powerful applications of certain passages of Holy Writ, in cases of perplexity, and as to his minute and confident explanations of the designs of Providence in the circumstances which happened to him, they are before the reader, who will peruse the whole account with such caution as he may deem requisite. *Valeat quantum valere potest.*[1] The Poet's peculiar cast of mind might possibly render him liable to be carried away, in some cases, by strong impressions of this kind, farther than a due regard to the Sacred Scriptures would exactly warrant. At the same time, obstinate incredulity on such subjects is not less bigoted and unreasonable than an undistinguishing faith. The opposite error to that, into which some may think that COWPER was occasionally betrayed—the error of those who entirely *overlook* the Providence of God—is more common, more foolish, and more pernicious. There is much unquestionable truth in the reflection which the illustrious writer of the Memoir thus expresses in one of his letters: "A thread of mercy ran through all the intricate maze of those afflictive providences, so mysterious to myself at the time, and which must ever remain so to all, who will not see what was the great design of them."

What COWPER meant by the *great design* to which he thus alludes, he has more plainly stated, in his Poem on Retirement; a short extract from which may not improperly conclude this Preface. Should it be perused by any individual, who is walking in paths of sorrow, similar to those with which the Poet was familiar, let him learn from a fellow-sufferer where he may find effectual solace. Let him be instructed, that, as COWPER elsewhere says, "Joy of heart is the best of all nervous medicines"; and that

1 Latin for "it shall have effect as far as it can have effect."

true "joy of heart" is only to be found in the knowledge of GOD, and of JESUS CHRIST whom he hath
sent. The passage, just mentioned, is the following:

And thou, sad sufferer under nameless ill,
That yields not to the touch of human skill,
Improve the kind occasion, understand
A Father's frown, and kiss his chastening hand.
To thee the day-spring and the blaze of noon,
The purple evening, and resplendent moon,
The stars that, sprinkled o'er the vault of night,
Seem drops descending in shower of light,
Shine not, or undesir'd and hated shine,
Seen through the medium of a cloud like thine.
Yet SEEK HIM; in his favour life is found,
All bliss beside a shadow or a sound;
Then heaven, eclipsed so long, and this dull earth,
Shall seem to start into second birth;
Nature, assuming a more lovely face,
Borrowing a beauty from the works of grace,
Shall be despised and overlooked no more,
Shall fill thee with delights unfelt before,
Impart to things inanimate a voice,
And bid her mountains and her hills rejoice;
The sound shall run along the winding vales,
And thou enjoy an Eden, ere it fails.[1]

LONDON, JULY 4, 1816.

---

1 A quote from *Retirement* by William Cowper.

# Memoir of
# the Early Life of
# William Cowper

I cannot recollect, that till the month of December, in the thirty-second year of my life, I had ever any serious impressions of the religious kind, or at all bethought myself of the things of my salvation, except in two or three instances. The first was of so transitory a nature, and passed when I was so very young, that, did I not intend what follows for a history of my heart, so far as religion has been its object, I should hardly mention it.

At six years old I was taken from the nursery, and from the immediate care of a most indulgent mother, and sent to a considerable school in Bedfordshire. Here I had hardships of different kinds to conflict with, which I felt more sensibly, in proportion to the tenderness with which I had been treated at home. But my chief affliction consisted in my being singled out from all the other boys, by a lad about fifteen years of age, as a proper object upon whom he might let loose the cruelty of his temper. I choose to forbear a particular recital of the many acts of barbarity, with which he made it his business continually to persecute me: it will be sufficient to say that he had, by his savage treatment of me, impressed such a dread of his figure upon my mind, that I well remember being afraid to lift up my eyes upon him, higher than his knees; and that I knew him by his shoe-buckles, better than any other part of his dress. May the Lord pardon him, and may we meet in glory!

One day as I was sitting alone on a bench in the school, melancholy, and almost ready to weep at the recollection of what I had already suffered, and expecting at the same time my tormentor every moment, these words of the Psalmist came into my mind, "I will not be afraid of what man can do unto me."[1] I applied this to my own case, with a degree of trust and confidence in God, that would have been no disgrace to a much more experienced Christian. Instantly I perceived in myself a briskness of spirits, and a cheerfulness, which I had never before experienced; and took several paces up and down the room with joyful alacrity—*his* gift in whom I trusted. Happy had it been for me, if this early effort towards a dependence on the blessed God had been frequently repeated by me. But, alas! it was the first and last instance of the kind, between infancy

1 Psalm 56:4.

and manhood. The cruelty of this boy, which he had long practiced in so secret a manner that no creature suspected it, was at length discovered. He was expelled from the school, and I was taken from it.

From hence, at eight years old, I was sent to Mr. D. an eminent surgeon and oculist, having very weak eyes, and being in danger of losing one of them. I continued a year in this family, where religion was neither known nor practiced; and from thence was dispatched to Westminster. Whatever seeds of religion I might carry thither, before my seven years' apprenticeship to the classics was expired, they were all marred and corrupted. The duty of the school-boy swallowed up every other; and I acquired Latin and Greek at the expense of a knowledge much more important.

Here occurred the second instance of serious consideration. As I was crossing St. Margaret's Church-yard, late one evening, I saw a glimmering light in the midst of it, which excited my curiosity. Just as I arrived at the spot, a grave-digger, who was at work by the light a his lanthorn, threw up a scull which struck me upon the leg. This little incident was an alarm to my conscience; for that evening may be remembered among the best religious documents which I received at Westminster. The impression, however, presently went off, and I became so forgetful of mortality, that, strange as it may seem, surveying my activity and strength, and, observing the evenness of my pulse, I began to entertain, with no small complacency, a notion, that perhaps I might never die! This notion was, however, very short-lived; for I was soon after struck with a lowness of spirits, uncommon at my age, and frequently had intimations of a consumptive habit. I had skill enough to understand their meaning, but could never prevail upon myself to disclose them to any one; for I thought any bodily infirmity a disgrace, especially a consumption. This messenger of the Lord, however, did his errand, and perfectly convinced me I was mortal.

That I may do justice to the place of my education, I must relate one mark of religious discipline, which, in my time, was observed at Westminster; I mean the pains which Dr. Nicholls took to prepare us for confirmation. The old man acquitted himself of this duty, like one who had a deep sense of its importance; and I believe most of us were struck by his manner, and affected by his exhortation. For my own part, I then, for the first time, attempted prayer in secret; but being little accustomed to that exercise of the heart, and having very childish notions of religion, I found it a difficult, and painful task; and was even then frightened at my own insensibility. This difficulty, though it did not subdue my good purposes, till the ceremony of confirmation was past, soon after entirely conquered them. I relapsed into a total forgetfulness of God, with the usual disadvantage of being more hardened, for having been softened to no purpose.

At twelve or thirteen, I was seized with the small-pox. I only mention this to show that at that early age, my heart was become proof against the ordinary means which a gracious God employs for our chastisement. Though I was severely handled by the disease, and in imminent danger; yet neither in the course of it, nor during my recovery, had I any sentiment of contrition, any thought of God or eternity. On the contrary, I was scarcely raised from the bed of pain and sickness, before the emotions of sin became more violent in me than ever; and the devil seemed rather to have gained than lost an advantage over me; so readily did I admit his suggestions, and so passive was I under them.

By this time, I became such an adept in the infernal art of lying, that I was seldom guilty of a fault, for which I could not, at a very short notice, invent an apology, capable of deceiving the wisest. These, I know, are called school-boys' tricks; but a total depravity of principle, and the work of the father of lies, are universally at the bottom them.

At the age of eighteen, being tolerably furnished with grammatical knowledge, but as ignorant in all points of religion as the satchel at my back, I was taken from Westminster; and having spent about nine months at home, was sent to acquire the practice of the law with an attorney. There I might have lived and died, without hearing or seeing any thing that might remind me of a single Christian duty, had it not been that I was at liberty to spend my leisure time (which was well nigh all my time) at my uncle's, in Southampton Row. By this means, I had indeed an opportunity of seeing the inside of a church, whither I went with the family on Sundays, which probably I should otherwise never have seen.

At the expiration of this term, I became, in a manner, complete master of myself; and took possession of a complete set of chambers in the Temple, at the age of twenty-one. This being a critical season of my life, and one upon which much depended, it pleased my all-merciful Father in Christ Jesus, to give a check to my rash and ruinous career of wickedness at the very outset. I was struck, not long after my settlement in the Temple, with such a dejection of spirits, as none but they who have felt the same, can have the least conception of. Day and night I was upon the rack, lying down in horror, and rising up in despair. I presently lost all relish for those studies, to which I had before been closely attached; the classics had no longer any charms for me; I had need of something more salutary than amusement, but I had no one to direct me where to find it.

At length I met with Herbert's Poems; and, gothic and uncouth as they were, I yet found in them a strain of piety which I could not but admire.

This was the only author I had any delight in reading. I pored over him all day long; and though I found not in them what I might have found—a cure for my malady—yet it never seemed so much alleviated as while I was reading him. At length, I was advised by a very near and dear relative, to lay him aside; for he thought such an author more likely to nourish my disorder, than to remove it.

In this state of mind I continued near twelvemonth; when, having experienced the inefficacy of all human means, I at length betook myself to God in prayer; such is the rank which our Redeemer holds in our esteem, that we never resorted to him but in the last instance, when all creatures have failed to succor us! My hard heart was at length softened, and my stubborn knees brought to bow. I composed a set of prayers, and made frequent use of them. Weak as my faith was, the Almighty, who will not break the bruised reed, nor quench the smoking flax, was graciously pleased to hear me.

A change of scene was recommended to me; and I embraced an opportunity of going with some friends to Southampton, where I spent several months. Soon after our arrival we walked to a place called Freemantle, about a mile from the town; the morning was clear and calm; the sun shone bright upon the sea; and the country on the borders of it was the most beautiful I had ever seen. We sat down upon an eminence, at the end of that arm of the sea,

which runs between Southampton and the New
Forest. Here it was, that on a sudden, as if another
sun had been kindled that instant in the heavens,
on purpose to dispel sorrow and vexation of spirit, I
felt the weight of all my misery taken off; my heart
became light and joyful in a moment; I could have
wept with transport had I been alone. I must needs
believe that nothing less than the Almighty fiat
could have filled me with such inexpressible delight;
not by a gradual dawning of peace, but as it were,
with a flash of his life-giving countenance. I think
I remember something like a glow of gratitude to
the Father of mercies, for this unexpected blessing,
and that I ascribed it to his gracious acceptance of
my prayers. But Satan, and my own wicked heart,
quickly persuaded me that I was indebted, for my
deliverance, to nothing but a change of scene, and
the amusing varieties of the place. By this means
he turned the blessing into a poison; teaching me
to conclude, that nothing but a continued circle of
diversion, and indulgence of appetite, could secure
me from a relapse.

Upon this hellish principle, as soon as I returned
to London, I burnt my prayers, and away went all
thoughts of devotion and of dependence upon
God my Saviour. Surely it was of his mercy that
I was not consumed. Glory be to his grace! Two
deliverances from danger were experienced without
making any impression, having spent about twelve

years in the Temple, in an uninterrupted course of sinful indulgence, and my associates and companions being either, like myself, professed Christians, or professed infidels, I obtained, at length, so complete a victory over my conscience, that all remonstrances from that quarter were in vain, and in a manner silenced; though sometimes, indeed, a question would arise in my mind, whether it were safe to proceed any farther in a course so plainly and utterly condemned in the Word of God. I saw clearly that if the gospel were true, such a conduct must inevitably end in my destruction; but I saw not by what means I could change my Ethiopian complexion, or overcome such an inveterate habit of rebelling against God.

The next thing that occurred to me, at such a time, was a doubt whether the gospel were true or false. To this succeeded many an anxious wish for the decision of this important question; for I foolishly thought, that obedience would presently follow, were I but convinced that it was worth while to attempt it. Having no reason to expect a miracle, and not hoping to be satisfied with any thing less, I acquiesced, at length, in the force of that devilish conclusion, that the only course I could take to secure my present peace, was to wink hard against the prospect of future misery, and to resolve to banish all thoughts of a subject, upon which I thought to so little purpose. Nevertheless, when I was in the company of Deists, and heard the gospel blasphemed, I never failed to assert the truth of it with much vehemence of disputation; for which I was the better qualified, having been always an industrious and diligent inquirer into the evidences by which it was externally supported. I think I once went so far into a controversy of this kind, as to assert, that I would gladly submit to have my right hand cut off; so that I might but be enabled to live according to the gospel. Thus have I been employed, when half intoxicated, in vindicating the truth of scripture, while in the very act of rebellion against its dictates! Lamentable inconsistency of convinced judgment with an unsanctified heart! An inconsistency, indeed, evident to others as well as to myself, inasmuch as a deistical friend of mine, with whom I was disputing upon the subject, cut short the matter, by alleging, that if what I said were true, I was certainly damned by my own showing.

By this time my patrimony being well nigh spent, and there being no appearance that I should ever repair the damage, by a fortune of my own getting, I began to be a little apprehensive of approaching want. It was, I imagine, under some apprehensions of this kind, that I one day said to a friend of mine, if the clerk of the journals of the House of Lords should die, I had some hopes that my kinsman, who had the place in his disposal, would appoint me to succeed him. We both agreed, that the business of that place being transacted in private, would exactly suit me; and both expressed an earnest wish for his death, that I might be provided for. Thus did I covet, what God had commanded me not to covet, and involved myself in still deeper guilt, by doing it in the spirit of a murderer. It pleased the Lord to give me my heart's desire, and with it, an immediate punishment for my crime. The poor man died, and by his death, not only the clerkship of the journals became vacant, but it became necessary to appoint new officers to two other places, jointly, as deputies to Mr. De Grey, who at this time resigned. These were the office of reading clerk, and the clerkship of the committees, of much greater value than that of the journals. The patentee of these appointments, (whom I pray to God to bless for his benevolent intention to serve me) called on me at my chambers, and having invited me to take a turn with him in the garden, there made me an offer of the two most profitable places; intending the other for his friend Mr. A.

Dazzled by so splendid a proposal, and not immediately reflecting upon my incapacity to execute a business of so public a nature, I at once accepted it; but at the same time, (such was the will of Him whose hand was in the whole matter) seemed to receive a dagger in my heart. The wound was given, and every moment added to the smart of it. All the considerations, by which I endeavored to compose my mind to its former tranquillity, did but torment me the more; proving miserable comforters and counsellors of no value. I returned to my chambers thoughtful and unhappy; my countenance fell; and my friend was astonished, instead of that additional cheerfulness he might so reasonably expect, to find an air of deep melancholy in all I said or did.

Having been harassed in this manner by day and night, for the space of a week, perplexed between the apparent folly of casting away the only visible chance I had of being well provided for, and the impossibility of retaining it, I determined at length to write a letter to my friend, though he lodged in a manner at the next door, and we generally spent the day together. I did so, and therein begged him to accept my resignation, and to appoint Mr. A. to the places he had given me; and permit me to succeed Mr. A. I was well aware of the disproportion between the value of his appointment and mine; but my peace was gone; pecuniary advantages were not equivalent to what I had lost; and I flattered myself, that the clerkship of the journals would fall fairly and easily within the scope of my abilities. Like a man in a fever, I thought a change of posture would relieve my pain; and as the event will show, was equally disappointed. At length I carried my point; my friend, in this instance, preferring the gratification of my desires to his own interest; for nothing could be so likely to bring a suspicion of bargain and sale upon his nomination, which the Lords would not have endured, as the appointment of so near a relative to the least profitable office, while the most valuable one was allotted to a stranger. The matter being thus settled, something like a calm took place in my mind.

I was, indeed, not a little concerned about my character, being aware, that it must needs suffer, by the strange appearance of my proceeding. This, however, being but a small part of the anxiety I had labored under, was hardly felt, when the rest was taken off. I thought my path towards an easy maintenance was now plain and open, and for a day or two was tolerably cheerful. But, behold, the storm was gathering all the while; and the fury of it was not the less violent from this gleam of sunshine.

In the beginning, a strong opposition to my friend's right of nomination began to show itself. A powerful party was formed among the Lords to thwart it, in favor of an old enemy to the family, though one much indebted to his bounty; and it appeared plain, that if we succeeded at last, it would only be by fighting our ground by inches. Every advantage, I was told, would be sought for, and eagerly seized, to disconcert us. I was bid to expect an examination at the bar of the House, touching my sufficiency for the post I had taken. Being necessarily ignorant of the nature of that business,

it became expedient, that I should visit the office
daily, is order to qualify myself for the strictest
scrutiny. All the horror of my fears and perplexi-
ties now returned. A thunderbolt would have been
as welcome to me, as this intelligence. I knew, to
demonstration, that upon these terms, the clerkship
of the journals was no place for me. To require my
attendance at the bar of the House, that I might
there publicly entitle myself to the office, was, in
effect, to exclude me from it. In the mean time, the
interest of my friend, the honor of his choice, and
my own reputation and circumstances, all urged
me forward; all pressed me to undertake that which
I saw to be impracticable. They whose spirits are
formed like mine, to whom a public exhibition of
themselves, on any occasion, is mortal poison, may
have some idea of the horror of my situation; others
can have none.

My continual misery at length brought on a
nervous fever: quiet forsook me by day, and peace
by night; a finger raised against me, was more than
I could stand against. In this posture of mind, I
attended regularly at the office; where, instead of
a soul upon the rack, the most active spirits were
essentially necessary for my purpose. I expected
no assistance from any one there, all the inferior
clerks being under the influence of my opponent;
and accordingly I received none. The journal books
were indeed thrown open to me; a thing which

could not be refused; and from which, perhaps, a man in health, and with a head turned to business, might have gained all the information he wanted. But it was not so with me. I read without perception, and was so distressed, that had every clerk in the office been my friend, it could have availed me little; for I was not in a condition to receive instruction, much less to elicit it out of manuscripts, without direction. Many months went over me thus employed; constant in the use of means, despairing as to the issue.

The feelings of a man, when he arrives at the place of execution, are, probably, much like mine, every time I set my foot in the office, which was every day, for more than half a year together.

At length the vacation being pretty far advanced, I made shift to get into the country, and repaired to Margate. There, by the help of cheerful company, a new scene, and the intermission of my painful employment, I presently began to recover my spirits; though even here, for some time after my arrival, (notwithstanding, perhaps, the preceding day had been spent agreeably, and without any disturbing recollection of my circumstances) my first reflections, when I awoke in the morning, were horrible, and full of wretchedness. I looked forward to the approaching winter, and regretted the flight of every moment, which brought it nearer; like a man borne away, by a rapid torrent, into a stormy sea, whence he sees no possibility of returning, and where he knows he cannot subsist. At length, indeed, I acquired such a facility of turning away my thoughts from the ensuing crisis, that, for weeks together, I hardly adverted to it at all. But the stress of the tempest was yet to come, and was not to be avoided by any resolution of mine to look another way.

"How wonderful are the works of the Lord, and his ways past finding out!" Thus was he preparing me for an event, which I had least of all expected, even the reception of his blessed gospel, working by means which, in all human contemplation, must needs seem directly opposite to that purpose, but which, in his wise and gracious disposal, have, I trust, effectually accomplished it.

About the beginning of October, 1763, I was again required to attend the office, and to prepare for the push. This no sooner took place, than all my misery returned. Again I visited the scene of ineffectual labors; again I felt myself pressed by necessity on either side, with nothing but despair in prospect. To this dilemma was I reduced, either to keep possession of the office to the last extremity, and by so doing, expose myself to a public rejection for insufficiency (for the little knowledge I had acquired, would have quite forsaken me at the bar of the House) or else to fling it up at once and by this means ran the hazard of ruining my benefactor's right of appointment, by bringing his discretion into question. In this situation, such a fit of passion has sometimes seized me, when alone in my chambers, that I have cried out aloud, and cursed the hour of my birth; lifting up my eyes to heaven, at the same time, not as a suppliant, but in the hellish spirit of rancorous reproach and blasphemy against my Maker. A thought would sometimes come across my mind, that my sins had perhaps brought this distress upon me, that the hand of divine vengeance was in it; but in the pride of my heart, I presently acquitted myself, and thereby implicitly charged God with injustice, saying, "What sins have I committed to deserve this?"

I saw plainly that God alone could deliver me; but was firmly persuaded that he would not, and therefore omitted to ask it. Ask it indeed at *his* hands, I would not; but as Saul sought to the witch; so did I to the physician, Dr. Heberden; and was as diligent in the use of drugs, as if they would have healed my wounded spirit, or have made the rough places plain before me. I made indeed, one effort of a devotional kind; for having found a prayer or two, I said them a few nights, but with so little expectation of prevailing that way, that I soon laid aside the book, and with it all thoughts of God, and hopes of a remedy.

I now began to look upon madness as the only chance remaining. I had a strong kind of foreboding, that so it would one day fare with me; and I wished for it earnestly, and looked forward to it with impatient expectation. My chief fear was, that my senses would not fail me time enough to excuse my appearance at the bar of the House of Lords, which was the only purpose I wanted it to answer. Accordingly the day of decision drew near, and I was still in my senses; though in my heart I had formed many wishes, and by word of mouth expressed many expectations to the contrary.

Now came the grand temptation; the point to which Satan had all the while been driving me— the dark and hellish purpose of self-murder. I grew more sullen and reserved, fled from all society, even from my most intimate friends, and shut myself up in my chambers. The ruin of my fortune, the contempt of my relations and acquaintance, the prejudice I should do my patron, were all urged upon me with irresistible energy. Being reconciled to the apprehension of madness, I began to be reconciled to the apprehension of death. Though formerly, in my happiest hours, I had never been able to glance a single thought that way, without shuddering at the idea of dissolution, I now wished for it, and found myself but little shocked at the idea of procuring it myself. Perhaps, thought I, there is no God; or if there be, the scriptures may be false; if so, then God has no where forbidden suicide. I considered life as my property, and therefore at my own disposal.

Men of great name, I observed, had destroyed themselves, and the world still retained the profoundest respect for their memories.

But above all, I was persuaded to believe, that if the act were ever so unlawful, and even supposing Christianity to be true, my misery in hell itself would be more supportable. I well recollect too, that when I was about eleven years of age, my father desired me to read a vindication of self-murder, and give him my sentiments upon the question: I did so, and argued against it. My father heard my reasons, and was silent, neither approving nor disapproving; from whence I inferred, that he sided with the author against me; though all the time, I believe the true motive for his conduct was, that he wanted; if he could, to think favorably of the state of a departed friend, who had some years before destroyed himself, and whose death had struck him with the deepest affliction. But this solution of the matter never once occurred to me, and the circumstance now weighed mightily with me.

At this time, I fell into company, at a chop-house; with an elderly, well-looking gentleman, whom I had often seen there before, but had never spoken to; he began the discourse, and talked much of the miseries he had suffered. This opened my heart to him; I freely and readily took part in the conversation. At length, self-murder became the topic; and in the result, we agreed, that the only reason why some men were content to drag on their sorrows with them to the grave, and others were not, was, that the latter were endued with a certain indignant fortitude of spirit, teaching them to despise life, which the former wanted. Another person, whom I met at a tavern, told me, that he had made up his mind about that matter, and had no doubt of his liberty to die as he saw convenient; though by the way, the same person, who has suffered many and great afflictions since, is still alive. Thus were the emissaries of the throne of darkness let loose upon me. Blessed be the Lord, who has brought much good out of all this evil! This concurrence of sentiment in men of sense, unknown to each other, I considered as a satisfactory decision of the question; and determined to proceed accordingly.

One evening in November, 1763, as soon as it was dark, affecting as cheerful and unconcerned an air as possible, I went into as apothecary's shop, and asked for an half ounce phial of laudanum. The man seemed to observe me narrowly; but if he did, I managed my voice and countenance, so as is deceive him. The day that required my attendance at the bar of the House, being not yet come, and about a week distant, I kept my bottle close in my side-pocket, resolved to use it when I should be convinced there was no other way of escaping. This, indeed, seemed evident already; but I was willing to allow myself every possible chance of that sort, and to protract the horrid execution of my purpose, till the last moment. But Satan was impatient of delay.

The day before the period above mentioned arrived, being at Richards' Coffee House at breakfast, I read the newspaper, and in it a letter, which the further I perused it, the more closely it engaged my attention. I cannot now recollect the purport of it; but before I had finished it, it appeared demonstratively true to me, that it was a libel, or satire, upon me. The author appeared to be acquainted with my purpose of self-destruction, and to have written that letter on purpose to secure and hasten, the execution of it. My mind, probably, at this time, began to be disordered. However it was, I was certainly given up to a strong delusion. I said within myself, "Your cruelty shall be gratified; you shall have your revenge"; and, flinging down the paper in a fit of strong passion, I rushed hastily out of the room, directing my steps towards the fields, where I intended to find some house to die in; or, if not, determined to poison myself in a ditch, when I should meet with one sufficiently retired.

Before I had walked a mile in the fields, a thought struck me, that I might yet spare my life— that I had nothing to do, but to sell what I had in the funds, (which might be done in an hour) go on board a ship, and transport myself to France. There, when every other way of maintenance should fail, I promised myself a comfortable asylum in some monastery, an acquisition easily made, by changing my religion. Not a little pleased with this expedient, I returned to my chambers, to pack up all that I could at so short a notice; but while I was looking over my portmanteau, my mind changed again, and self-murder was recommended to me, once more, in all its advantages.

Not knowing where to poison myself, for I was liable to continual interruption in my chambers, from my laundress and her husband, I laid aside that intention, and resolved upon drowning. For that purpose, I immediately took a coach, and ordered the man to drive to the Tower Wharf, intending to throw myself into the river, from the Custom-house Quay. It would be strange, should I omit to observe here, how I was continually hurried away from such places as were most favorable to my design, to others, where it was almost impossible to execute it; from the fields, where it was improbable that any thing should happen to prevent me, to the Custom-house Quay, where every thing of that kind was to be expected; and this by a sudden impulse, which lasted just long enough to call me back again to my chambers, and which was then immediately withdrawn. Nothing ever appeared more feasible, than the project of going to France, till it had served its purpose, and then, in an instant, it appeared impracticable and absurd, even to a degree of ridicule.

My life, which I had called my own, and claimed as a right to dispose of, was kept for me by him whose property indeed it was, and who alone had a right to dispose of it. This is not the only occasion on which it is proper to make this remark; others will offer themselves in the course of this narrative, so fairly, that the reader cannot overlook them.

I left the coach upon the Tower Wharf, intending never to return to it; but upon coming to the Quay, I found the water low, and a porter seated upon some goods there, as if on purpose to prevent me. This passage to the bottomless pit being mercifully shut against me, I returned to the coach, and ordered the man to drive back again to the Temple. I drew up the shutters, once more had recourse to the laudanum, and determined to drink it off directly; but God had otherwise ordained. A conflict that shook me to pieces suddenly took place; not properly a trembling, but a convulsive agitation, which deprived me in a manner of the use of my limbs: and my mind was as much shaken as my body.

Distracted between the desire of death, and the dread of it, twenty times I had the phial to my mouth, and as often received an irresistible check; and even at the time it seemed to me, that an invisible hand swayed the bottle downwards, as often as I set it against my lips. I well remember, that I took notice of this circumstance with some surprise, though it effected no change in my purpose.

Panting for breath, and in an horrible agony, I flung myself back into a corner of the coach. A few drops of the laudanum, which had touched my lips, besides the fumes of it, began to have a stupefying effect upon me. Regretting the loss of so fair an opportunity, yet utterly unable to avail myself of it, I determined not to live; and, already half dead with anguish, I once more returned to the Temple. Instantly I repaired to my room, and having shut both the outer and inner door, prepared myself for the last scene of the tragedy. I poured the laudanum into a small basin, set it on a chair by the bedside, half undressed myself, and laid down between the blankets, shuddering with horror at what I was about to perpetrate.—I reproached myself bitterly with folly and rank cowardice, for having suffered the fear of death to influence me as it had done, and was filled with disdain at my own pitiful timidity: but still something seemed to overrule me, and to say, *"Think what you are doing!—Consider, and live."*

At length, however, with the most confirmed resolution, I reached forth my hand towards the basin, when the fingers of both hands were so closely contracted, as if bound with a cord, and became entirely useless. Still, indeed, I could have made shift with both hands, dead and lifeless as they were, to have raised the basin to my mouth; for my arms were not at all affected. But this new difficulty struck me with wonder; it had the air of a divine interposition. I lay down in bed again to muse upon it; and while thus employed, I heard the key turn in the outer door, and my laundress's husband came in. By this time the use of my fingers was restored to me: I started up hastily—dressed myself, hid the basin; and, affecting as composed an air as I could, walked out into dining-room. In a few minutes I was left alone; and now, unless God had evidently interposed for my preservation, I should certainly have done execution upon myself, having a whole afternoon before me.

Both the man and his wife being gone, outward obstructions were no sooner removed, than new ones arose within. The man had just shut the door behind him, when the convincing Spirit came upon me, and a total alteration in my sentiments took place. The horror of the crime was immediately exhibited to me in so strong a light, that, being seized with a kind of furious indignation, I snatched up the basin, poured away the laudanum into a phial of foul water, and, not content with that, flung the phial out of the window. This impulse, having served the present purpose, was withdrawn.

I spent the rest of the day in a kind of stupid insensibility; undetermined as to the manner of dying, but still bent on self-murder, as the only possible deliverance. That sense of the enormity of the crime, which I had just experienced, had entirely left me; and, unless my Eternal Father in Christ Jesus had interposed to disannul my covenant with death, and my agreement with hell, that I might hereafter be admitted into the covenant of mercy, I had, by this time, been a companion of devils, and the just object of his boundless vengeance.

In the evening, a most intimate friend called upon me, and felicitated me on a happy resolution, which he had heard I had taken, to stand the brunt, and keep the office. I knew not whence this intelligence arose, but did not contradict it. We conversed awhile, with a real cheerfulness on his part, and an affected one on mine; and when he left me, I said in my heart, I shall see thee no more!

Behold, into what extremities a *good sort of man* may fall! Such was I, in the estimation of those who knew me best: a decent outside is all a good-natured world requires. Thus equipped, though all within be rank atheism, rottenness of heart, and rebellion against the blessed God, we are said to be good enough; and if *we* are damned, alas! who shall be saved! Reverse this charitable reflection, and say, If *a good sort of man* be saved, who then shall perish; and it comes much nearer the truth: but this is a hard saying, and the world cannot bear it.

I went to bed, as I thought, to take my last sleep in this world. The next morning was to place me at the bar of the House, and I determined not to see it.

I slept as usual, and awoke about three o'clock. Immediately I arose, and by the help of a rush-light, found my penknife, took it into bed with me, and lay with it for some hours directly pointed against my heart. Twice, or thrice, I placed it upright under my left breast, leaning all my weight upon it; but the point was broken off, and would not penetrate.

In this manner the time passed till the day began to break. I heard the clock strike seven, and instantly it occurred to me, there was no time to be lost: the chambers would soon be opened, and my friend would call upon me to take me with him to Westminster. "Now is the time," thought I, "this is the crisis; no more dallying with the love of life." I arose, and, as I thought, bolted the inner door of my chambers, but was mistaken; my touch deceived me, and I left it as I found it. My preservation, indeed, as it will appear, did not depend upon that incident; but I mention it, to show, that the good providence of God watched over me, to keep open every way of deliverance, that nothing might be left to hazard.

Not one hesitating thought now remained; but I fell greedily to the execution of my purpose. My garter was made of a broad scarlet binding, with a sliding buckle, being sewn together at the ends: by the help of the buckle, I made a noose, and fixed it about my neck, straining it so tight, that I hardly left a passage for my breath, or for the blood to circulate; the tongue of the buckle held it fast. At each corner of the bed, was placed a wreath of carved work, fastened by an iron pin, which passed up through the midst of it. The other part of the garter, which made a loop, I slipped over one of these, and hung by it some seconds, drawing up my feet under me, that they might not touch the floor; but the iron bent, the carved work slipped off, and the garter with it. I then fastened it to the frame of the tester, winding it round, and tying it in a strong knot. The frame broke short, and let me down again.

The third effort was more likely to succeed. I set the door open, which reached within a foot of the ceiling; by the help of a chair I could command the top of it, and the loop being large enough to admit a large angle of the door, was easily fixed, so as not to slip off again. I pushed away the chair with my feet, and hung at my whole length. While I hung there, I distinctly heard a voice say three times, "*'Tis over!*"

Though I am sure of the fact, and was so at the time, yet it did not at all alarm me, or affect my resolution. I hung so long, that I lost all sense, all consciousness of existence.

When I came to myself again, I thought myself in hell; the sound of my own dreadful groans was all that I heard, and a feeling, like that of flashes, was just beginning to seize upon my whole body. In a few seconds, I found myself fallen with my face to the floor. In about half a minute, I recovered my feet; and reeling, and staggering, I stumbled into bed again.

By the blessed providence of God, the garter which had held me till the bitterness of temporal death was past, broke, just before eternal death had taken place upon me. The stagnation of the blood under one eye, in a broad crimson spot, and a red circle about my neck, showed plainly that I had been on the brink of eternity. The latter, indeed, might have been occasioned by the pressure of the garter; but the former was certainly the effect of strangulation; for it was not attended with the sensation of a bruise, as it must have been, had I, in my fall, received one in so tender a part. And I rather think the circle round my neck was owing to the same cause; for the part was not excoriated, nor at all in pain.

Soon after I got into bed, I was surprised to hear a noise in the dining-room, where the laundress was lighting a fire; she had found the door unbolted, notwithstanding my design to fasten it, and must have passed the bed-chamber door while I was hanging on it, and yet never perceived me. She heard me fall, and presently came to ask if I was well; adding, she feared I had been in a fit.

I sent her to a friend, to whom I related the whole affair, and dispatched him to my kinsman, at the coffee-house. As soon as the latter arrived,

I pointed to the broken garter, which lay in the middle of the room; and apprised him also of the attempt I had been making.—His words were, "My dear Mr. Cowper, you terrify me; to be sure you cannot hold the office at this rate—where is the deputation?" I gave him the key of the drawers, where it was deposited; and his business requiring his immediate attendance, he took it away with him; and thus ended all my connection with the Parliament House.

To this moment I had felt no concern of a spiritual kind. Ignorant of original sin, insensible of the guilt of actual transgression, I understood neither the law nor the gospel; the condemning nature of the one, nor the restoring mercies of the other. I was as much unacquainted with Christ, in all his saving offices, as if his blessed name had never reached me. Now, therefore, a new scene opened upon me. Conviction of sin took place, especially of that just committed; the meanness of it, as well as its atrocity, were exhibited to me in colors so inconceivably strong, that I despised myself, with a contempt not to be imagined or expressed, for having attempted it. This sense of it secured me from the repetition of a crime, which I could not now reflect on without abhorrence.

Before I arose from bed, it was suggested to me, that there was nothing wanted but murder, to fill up the measure of my iniquities; and that, though I had failed in my design, yet I had all the guilt of that crime to answer for. A sense of God's wrath, and a deep despair of escaping it, instantly succeeded. The fear of death became much more prevalent in me than ever the desire of it had been.

A frequent flashing, like that of fire, before my eyes, and an excessive pressure upon the brain, made me apprehensive of an apoplexy; an event which I thought the more probable, as an extravasation in that part seemed likely enough to happen, in so violent a struggle.

By the advice of my dear friend and benefactor, who called upon me again at noon, I sent for a physician, and told him the fact, and the stroke I apprehended. He assured me, there was no danger of it, and advised me, by all means, to retire into the country. Being made easy in that particular, and not knowing where to better myself, I continued in my chambers, where the solitude of my situation left me at full liberty to attend to my spiritual state; a matter I had, till this day, never sufficiently thought of.

At this time I wrote to my brother, at Cambridge, to inform him of the distress I had been in, and the dreadful method I had taken to deliver myself from it; assuring him, as I faithfully might, that I had laid aside all such horrid intentions, and was desirous to live as long as it would please the Almighty to permit me.

My sins were now set in array against me, and I

began to see and feel that I had lived without God in the world. As I walked to and fro in my chamber, I said within myself, "There never was so abandoned a wretch; so great a sinner." All my worldly sorrows seemed as though they had never been; the terrors which succeeded them seemed so great, and so much more afflicting. One moment I thought myself shut out from mercy, by one chapter; the next, by another. The sword of the Spirit seemed to guard the tree of life from my touch, and to flame against me in every avenue by which I attempted to approach it. I particularly remember, that the parable of the barren fig-tree was to me an inconceivable source of anguish; and I applied it to myself, with a strong persuasion in my mind, that when the Saviour pronounced a curse upon it, he had me in his eye; and pointed that curse directly at me.

I turned over all Archbishop Tillotson's sermons, in hopes to find one upon the subject, and consulted my brother upon the true meaning of it; desirous, if possible, to obtain a different interpretation of the matter, than my evil conscience would suffer me to fasten on it. "O Lord, thou didst vex me with all thy storms, all thy billows went over me; thou didst run upon me like a giant in the night season, thou didst scare me with visions in the night season."

In every book I opened, I found something that struck me to the heart. I remember taking up a volume of Beaumont and Fletcher, which lay upon the table in my kinsman's lodgings, and the first sentence which I saw was this: "The justice of the gods is in it." My heart instantly replied, "It is a truth," and I cannot but observe, that as I found something in every author to condemn me, so it was the first sentence, in general, I pitched upon. Every thing preached to me, and every thing preached the curse of the law.

I was now strongly tempted to use laudanum, not as a poison, but as an opiate, to compose my spirits; to stupefy my awakened and feeling mind; harassed with sleepless nights, and days of uninterrupted misery. But God forbad it, who would have nothing to interfere with the quickening work he had begun in me; and neither the want of rest, nor continued agony of mind, could bring me to the use of it: I hated and abhorred the very smell of it.

I never went into the street, but I thought the people stood and laughed at me, and held me in contempt; and could hardly persuade myself, but that the voice of my conscience was loud enough for every one to hear it. They who knew me, seemed to avoid me; and if they spoke to me, seemed to do it in scorn. I bought a ballad of one who was singing it in the street, because I thought it was written on me.

I dined alone, either at the tavern, where I went in the dark, or at the chop-house, where I always took care to hide myself in the darkest corner of the room. I slept generally an hour in the evening; but it was only to be terrified in dreams; and when I awoke, it was some time before I could walk steadily through the passage into the dining-room. I reeled and staggered like a drunken man; the eyes of man I could not bear; but when I thought that the eyes of God were upon me (which I felt assured of) it gave me the most intolerable anguish. If, for a moment, a book or a companion, stole away my attention from myself, a flash from hell seemed to be thrown into my mind immediately; and I said within myself, "What are these things to me, who am damned?" In a word, I saw myself a sinner altogether, and every way a sinner; but I saw not yet a glimpse of the mercy of God in Jesus Christ.

The capital engine in all the artillery of Satan had not yet been employed against me; already overwhelmed with despair, I was not yet sunk into the bottom of the gulf. This was a fit season for the use of it; and accordingly I was set to inquire, whether I had not been guilty of the unpardonable sin; and was presently persuaded that I had.

A neglect to improve the mercies of God at Southampton, on the occasion above mentioned, was represented to me as the sin against the Holy Ghost. No favorable construction of my conduct in that instance; no argument of my brother's, who was now with me; nothing he could suggest, in extenuation of my offenses, could gain a moment's admission. Satan furnished me so readily with weapons against myself, that neither scripture nor reason could undeceive me. Life appeared to me now more eligible than death, only because it was a barrier between me and everlasting burnings.

My thoughts in the day became still more gloomy, and my night visions more dreadful. One morning, as I lay between sleeping and waking, I seemed to myself to be walking in Westminster Abbey, waiting till prayers should begin; presently I thought I heard the minister's voice, and hastened towards the choir; just as I was upon the point of entering, the iron gate under the organ was flung in my face, with a jar that made the Abbey ring; the noise awoke me; and a sentence of excommunication from all the churches upon earth could not have been so dreadful to me, as the interpretation which I could not avoid putting upon this dream.

Another time I seemed to pronounce to myself, "Evil be thou my good." I verily thought that I had adopted that hellish sentiment, it seemed to come so directly from my heart. I rose from bed, to look for my prayer-book, and having found it, endeavored to pray; but immediately experienced the impossibility of drawing nigh to God, unless he first draw nigh to us. I made many passionate attempts towards prayer, but failed in all.

Having an obscure notion about the efficacy of faith, I resolved upon an experiment, to prove whether I had faith or not. For this purpose, I resolved to repeat the Creed; when I came to the second period of it, all traces of the former were struck out of my memory, nor could I recollect one syllable of the matter. While I endeavored to recover it, and when just upon the point, I perceived a sensation in my brain, like a tremulous vibration in all the fibers of it. By this means, I lost the words in the very instant when I thought to have laid hold of them. This threw me into an agony; but growing a little calmer, I made an attempt for the third time; here again I failed in the same manner as before.

I considered it as a supernatural interposition, to inform me, that having sinned against the Holy Ghost, I had no longer any interest in Christ, or in the gifts of the Spirit. Being assured of this, with the most rooted conviction, I gave myself up to despair. I felt a sense of burning in my heart, like that of real fire, and concluded it was an earnest of those eternal flames which would soon receive me. I laid myself down, howling with horror, while my knees smote against each other.

In this condition my brother found me, and the first words I spoke to him were, "Oh! Brother, I am damned! think of eternity, and then think what it is to be damned!" I had, indeed, a sense of eternity impressed upon my mind, which seemed almost to amount to a full comprehension of it.

My brother, pierced to the heart with the sight

of my misery, tried to comfort me; but all to no purpose. I refused comfort, and my mind appeared to me in such colors, that to administer it to me, was only to exasperate me, and to mock my fears.

At length, I remembered my friend Martin Madan, and sent for him. I used to think him an enthusiast, but now seemed convinced, that if there was any balm in Gilead, he must administer it to me. On former occasions, when my spiritual concerns had at any time occurred to me, I thought likewise on the necessity of repentance. I knew that many persons had spoken of shedding tears for sin; but when I asked myself, whether the time would ever come, when I should weep for mine, it seemed to me that a stone might sooner do it.

Not knowing that Christ was exalted to give repentance, I despaired of ever attaining to it. My friend came to me; we sat on the bedside together, and he began to declare to me the gospel. He spoke of original sin, and the corruption of every man born into the world, whereby every one is a child of wrath. I perceived something like hope dawning in my heart. This doctrine set me more on a level with the rest of mankind, and made my condition appear less desperate.

Next he insisted on the all-atoning efficacy of the blood of Jesus, and his righteousness, for our justification. While I heard this part of his discourse, and the scriptures on which he founded it, my heart began to burn within me; my soul was pierced with a sense of my bitter ingratitude to so merciful a Saviour; and those tears, which I thought impossible, burst forth freely. I saw clearly, that my case required such a remedy, and had not the least doubt within me, but that this was the gospel of salvation.

Lastly, he urged the necessity of a lively faith in Jesus Christ; not an assent only of the understanding, but a faith of application, an actually laying hold of it, and embracing it as a salvation wrought out for me personally. Here I failed, and deplored my want of such a faith. He told me it was the gift of God, which he trusted he would bestow upon me. I could only reply, "I wish he would": a very irreverent petition; but a very sincere one, and such as the blessed God, in his due time, was pleased to answer.

My brother, finding that I had received consolation from Mr. Madan, was very anxious, that I should take the earliest opportunity of conversing with him again; and for this purpose, pressed me to go to him immediately. I was for putting it off; but my brother seemed impatient of delay; and, at length, prevailed on me to set out. I mention this, to the honor of his candor and humanity; which would suffer no difference of sentiments to interfere with them. My welfare was his only object, and all prejudices fled before his zeal to procure it. May he receive, for his recompense, all that happiness the gospel, which I then first became acquainted with, is alone able to impart!

Easier, indeed, I was; but far from easy. The wounded spirit within me was less in pain, but by no means healed. What I had experienced was but the beginning of sorrows, and a long train of still greater terrors was at hand. I slept my three hours well, and then awoke with ten times a stronger alienation from God than ever.

Satan plied me closely with horrible visions, and more horrible voices. My ears rang with the sound of torments, that seemed to await me. Then did the pains of hell get hold on me, and, before daybreak, the very sorrows of death encompassed me. A numbness seized upon the extremities of my body, and life seemed to retreat before it; my hands and feet became cold and stiff; a cold sweat stood upon my forehead; my heart seemed at every pulse to beat its last, and my soul to cling to my lips, as if on the very brink of departure. No convicted criminal ever feared death more, or was more assured of dying.

At eleven o'clock, my brother called upon me, and in about an hour after his arrival, that distemper of mind, which I had so ardently wished for, actually seized me.

While I traversed the apartment, in the most horrible dismay of soul, expecting every moment, that the earth would open her mouth and swallow me; my conscience scaring me, the avenger of blood pursuing me, and the city of refuge out of reach and out of sight; a strange and horrible darkness fell upon me. If it were possible, that a heavy blow could light on the brain, without touching the skull, such was the sensation I felt. I clapped my hand to my forehead, and cried aloud, through the pain it gave me. At every stroke, my thoughts and expressions became more wild and incoherent; all that remained clear was the sense of sin, and the expectation of punishment. These kept undisturbed possession all through my illness, without interruption or abatement.

My brother instantly observed the change, and consulted with my friends on the best manner to dispose of me. It was agreed among them, that I should be carried to St. Alban's, where Dr. Cotton kept a house for the reception of such patients, and with whom I was known to have a slight acquaintance. Not only his skill, as a physician, recommended him to their choice, but his well-known humanity, and sweetness of temper. It will be proper to draw a veil over the secrets of my prison-house: let it suffice to say, that the low state of body and mind, to which I was reduced, was perfectly well calculated to humble the natural vain-glory and pride of my heart.

These are the efficacious means which Infinite

Wisdom thought meet to make use of for that purpose. A sense of self-loathing and abhorrence ran through all my insanity. Conviction of sin, and expectation of instant judgment, never left me, from the 7ᵀᴴ of December, 1763, until the middle of July following. The accuser of the brethren was ever busy with me night and day, bringing to my recollection in dreams the commission of long-forgotten sins, and charging upon my conscience things of an indifferent nature, as atrocious crimes.

All that passed in this long interval of eight months may be classed under two heads, conviction of sin, and despair of mercy. But, blessed be the God of my salvation for every sigh I drew, for every tear I shed; since thus it pleased him to judge me here, that I might not be judged hereafter.

After five months of continual expectation, that the divine vengeance would plunge me into the bottomless pit, I became so familiar with despair, as to have contracted a sort of hardiness and indifference as to the event. I began to persuade myself, that while the execution of the sentence was suspended, it would be for my interest to indulge a less horrible train of ideas, than I had been accustomed to muse upon. "Eat, and drink, for tomorrow thou shalt be in hell," was the maxim on which I proceeded. By this means, I entered into conversation with the Doctor, laughed at his stories, and told him some of my own to match them; still, however, carrying a sentence of irrevocable doom in my heart.

He observed the seeming alteration with plea-sure. Believing, as well he might, that my smiles were sincere, he thought my recovery well nigh completed; but they were, in reality, like the green surface of a morass, pleasant to the eye, but a cover for nothing but rottenness and filth. The only thing that could promote and effectuate my cure, was yet wanting—an experimental knowledge of the redemption which is in Christ Jesus.

I remember, about this time, a diabolical species of regret that found harbor in my wretched heart. I was sincerely sorry that I had not seized every opportunity of giving scope to my wicked appe-tites, and even envied those, who being departed to their own place before me, had the consolation to reflect, that they had well earned their miserable inheritance, by indulging their sensuality without restraint. Oh merciful God! What a tophet of pol-lution is the human soul, and wherein do we differ from the devils, unless thy grace prevent us!

In about three months more (July 25, 1764), my brother came from Cambridge to visit me. Dr. C. having told him that he thought me greatly amended, he was rather disappointed at finding me almost as silent and reserved as ever; for the first sight of him struck me with many painful sensa-tions both of sorrow for my own remediless condi-tion, and envy of his happiness.

As soon as we were left alone, he asked me how I found myself; I answered, "As much better as despair can make me." We went together into the garden. Here, on expressing a settled assurance of sudden judgment, he protested to me, that it was all a delusion; and protested so strongly, that I could not help giving some attention to him. I burst into tears, and cried out, "If it be a delusion, then am I the happiest of beings." Something like a ray of hope was shot into my heart; but still I was afraid to indulge it. We dined together, and I spent the afternoon in a more cheerful manner. Something seemed to whisper to me every moment, "Still there is mercy."

Even after he left me, this change of sentiment gathered ground continually; yet my mind was in such a fluctuating state, that I can only call it a vague presage of better things at hand, without being able to assign a reason for it. The servant observed a sudden alteration in me for the better; and the man, whom I have ever since retained in my service, expressed great joy on the occasion.

I went to bed and slept well. In the morning, I dreamed that the sweetest boy I ever saw came dancing up to my bedside; he seemed just out of leading-strings, yet I took particular notice of the firmness and steadiness of his tread. The sight affected me with pleasure, and served at least to harmonize my spirits; so that I awoke for the first time with a sensation of delight on my mind. Still, however, I knew not where to look for the establishment of the comfort I felt; my joy was as much a mystery to myself as to those about me. The blessed God was preparing me for the clearer light of his countenance by this first dawning of that light upon me.

Within a few days of my first arrival at St. Alban's, I had thrown aside the Word of God, as a book in which I had no longer any interest or portion. The only instance, in which I can recollect reading a single chapter, was about two months before my recovery. Having found a Bible on the bench in the garden, I opened upon the 11ᵀᴴ of St. John, where Lazarus is raised from the dead; and saw so much benevolence, mercy, goodness, and sympathy with miserable man, in our Saviour's conduct, that I almost shed tears even after the relation; little thinking that it was an exact type of the mercy which Jesus was on the point of extending towards myself. I sighed, and said, "Oh, that I had not rejected so good a Redeemer, that I had not forfeited all his favors!" Thus was my heart softened, though not yet enlightened. I closed the book, without intending to open it again.

Having risen with somewhat of a more cheerful feeling, I repaired to my room, where breakfast waited for me. While I sat at table, I found the cloud of horror, which had so long hung over me, was every moment passing away; and every moment came fraught with hope. I was continually more and more persuaded, that I was not utterly doomed to destruction. The way of salvation was still, however, hid from my eyes; nor did I see it at all clearer than before my illness. I only thought, that if it would please God to spare me, I would lead a better life; and that I would yet escape hell, if a religious observance of my duty would secure me from it.

Thus may the terror of the Lord make a Pharisee; but only the sweet voice of mercy in the gospel, can make a Christian.

But the happy period which was to shake off my fetters, and afford me a clear opening of the free mercy of God in Christ Jesus, was now arrived. I flung myself into a chair near the window, and seeing a Bible there, ventured once more to apply to it for comfort and instruction. The first verse I saw, was the 25TH of the 3RD of Romans: "Whom God hath set forth to be a propitiation through faith in his blood, to declare his righteousness for the remission of sins that are past, through the forbearance of God."

Immediately I received strength to believe it, and the full beams of the Sun of Righteousness shone upon me. I saw the sufficiency of the atonement he had made, my pardon sealed in his blood, and all the fullness and completeness of his justification. In a moment I believed, and received the gospel.

Whatever my friend Madan had said to me, long before, revived in all its clearness, with demonstration of the Spirit and with power. Unless the Almighty arm had been under me, I think I should have died with gratitude and joy. My eyes filled with tears, and my voice choked with transport, I could only look up to heaven in silent fear, overwhelmed with love and wonder. But the work of the Holy Ghost is best described in his own words. It is "joy unspeakable, and full of glory."[1] Thus was my heavenly Father in Christ Jesus pleased to give me the full assurance of faith, and out of a strong, stony, unbelieving heart, to raise up a child unto Abraham. How glad should I now have been to have spent every moment in prayer and thanksgiving!

I lost no opportunity of repairing to a throne of grace; but flew to it with an earnestness irresistible and never to be satisfied. Could I help it? Could I do otherwise than love and rejoice in my reconciled Father in Christ Jesus? The Lord had enlarged my heart, and I ran in the way of his commandments. For many succeeding weeks, tears were ready to flow, if I did but speak of the gospel, or mention the name of Jesus. To rejoice day and night was all my employment. Too happy to sleep much, I thought it was but lost time that was spent in slumber. Oh that the ardor of my first love had continued! But I have known many a lifeless and unhallowed hour

1  1 Peter 1:8.

since; long intervals of darkness, interrupted by short returns of peace and joy in believing.

My physician, ever watchful and apprehensive for my welfare, was now alarmed, lest the sudden transition from despair to joy, should terminate in a fatal frenzy. But "the Lord was my strength and my song, and was become my salvation."[1] I said, "I shall not die, but live, and declare the works of the Lord; he has chastened me sore, but not given me over unto death.[2] O give thanks unto the Lord, for his mercy endureth for ever."[3]

In a short time, Dr. C. became satisfied, and acquiesced in the soundness of my cure; and much sweet communion I had with him, concerning the things of our salvation. He visited me every morning while I stayed with him, which was near twelve months after my recovery, and the gospel was the delightful theme of our conversation.

No trial has befallen me since, but what might be expected in a state of warfare. Satan, indeed, has changed his battery. Before my conversion, sensual gratification was the weapon with which he sought to destroy me. Being naturally of an easy, quiet disposition, I was seldom tempted to anger; yet that passion it is which now gives me the most disturbance, and occasions the sharpest conflicts.

1 Psalm 118:14.
2 Psalm 118:17, 18.
3 Psalm 118:29.

But Jesus being my strength, I fight against it; and if I am not conqueror, yet I am not overcome.

I now employed my brother to seek out an abode for me in the neighborhood of Cambridge, being determined, by the Lord's leave, to see London, the scene of my former abominations, no more. I had still one place of preferment left, which seemed to bind me under the necessity of returning thither again. But I resolved to break the bond, chiefly because my peace of conscience was in question. I held, for some years, the office of commissioner of bankrupts, with about 60*l.* per annum. Conscious of my ignorance of the law, I could not take the accustomed oath, and resigned it; thereby releasing myself from an occasion of great sin, and every obligation to return to London. By this means, I reduced myself to an income scarcely sufficient for my maintenance; but I would rather have starved in reality, than deliberately offend against my Saviour; and his great mercy has since raised me up such friends, as have enabled me to enjoy all the comforts and conveniences of life. I am well assured, that while I live, "bread shall be given me, and water shall be sure,"[1] according to his gracious promise.

After my brother had made many unsuccessful attempts to procure me a dwelling near him, I one day poured out my soul in prayer to God, beseeching him, that wherever he should be pleased, in his

1  Isaiah 33:16.

fatherly mercy, to lead me, it might be in the society of those who feared his name, and loved the Lord Jesus Christ in sincerity; a prayer, of which I have good reason to acknowledge his gracious acceptance.

In the beginning of June, 1765, I received a letter from my brother, to say, he had taken lodgings for me at Huntingdon, which he believed would suit me. Though it was sixteen miles from Cambridge, I was resolved to take them; for I had been two months in perfect health; and my circumstances required a less expensive way of life. It was with great reluctance, however, that I thought of leaving the place of my second nativity; I had so much leisure there to study the blessed Word of God, and had enjoyed so much happiness; but God ordered every thing for me, like an indulgent Father, and had prepared a more comfortable place of residence, than I could have chosen for myself.

On the 7ᵀᴴ of June, 1765, having spent more than eighteen months at St. Alban's, partly in bondage, and partly in the liberty wherewith Christ had made me free, I took my leave of the place at four in the morning, and set out for Cambridge.

The servant, whom I lately mentioned as rejoicing in my recovery, attended me. He had maintained such an affectionate watchfulness over me during my whole illness, and waited on me with so much patience and gentleness, that I could not bear

to leave him behind, though it was with some difficulty the Doctor was prevailed on to part with him.
The strongest argument of all was the earnest desire
he expressed to follow me. He seemed to have been
providentially thrown in my way, having entered Dr.
C.'s service just time enough to attend me; and I
have strong ground to hope, that God will use me as
an instrument to bring him to a knowledge of Jesus.
It is impossible to say, with how delightful a sense of
his protection, and fatherly care of me, it has pleased
the Almighty to favor me, during the whole journey.

I remembered the pollution which is in the
world, and the sad share I had in it myself; and my
heart ached at the thought of entering it again. The
blessed God had endued me with some concern for
his glory, and I was fearful of hearing it traduced
by oaths and blasphemies, the common language of
this highly favored, but ungrateful country. But "fear
not, I am with thee," was my comfort. I passed the
whole journey in silent communion with God; and
these hours are amongst the happiest I have known.

I repaired to Huntingdon the Saturday after my
arrival at Cambridge. My brother, who had attended
me thither, had no sooner left me, than finding
myself surrounded by strangers, and in a strange
place, my spirits began to sink, and I felt (such was
the backslidings of my heart) like a traveller in the
midst of an inhospitable desert, without a friend to
comfort, or a guide to direct me. I walked forth,

towards the close of the day, in this melancholy frame of mind, and having wandered about a mile from the town, I found my heart, at length, so powerfully drawn towards the Lord, that having gained a retired and secret nook in the corner of a field, I kneeled down under a bank, and poured forth my complaints before him. It pleased my Saviour to hear me, in that this oppression was taken off, and I was enabled to trust in him that careth for the stranger, to roll my burden upon him, and to rest assured, that wheresoever he might cast my lot, the God of all consolation would still be with me. But this was not all. He did for me more than either I had asked or thought.

The next day, I went to church for the first time after my recovery. Throughout the whole service, I had much to do to restrain my emotions, so fully did I see the beauty and the glory of the Lord. My heart was full of love to all the congregation, especially to them, in whom I observed an air of sober attention. A grave and sober person sat in the pew with me; him I have since seen and often conversed with, and have found him a pious man, and a true servant of the blessed Redeemer. While he was singing the psalm, I looked at him, and observing him intent on his holy employment, I could not help saying in my heart, with much emotion, "Bless you, for praising him whom my soul loveth!"

Such was the goodness of the Lord to me, that

he gave me the oil of joy for mourning, and the garment of praise for the Spirit of heaviness; and though my voice was silent, being stopped by the intenseness of what I felt, yet my soul sung within me, and even leapt for joy. And when the gospel for the day was read, the sound of it was more than I could well support. Oh, what a word is the word of God, when the Spirit quickens us to receive it, and gives the hearing ear, and the understanding heart! The harmony of heaven is in it, and discovers its author. The parable of the prodigal son was the portion. I saw myself in that glass so clearly, and the loving kindness of my slighted and forgotten Lord, that the whole scene was realized to me, and acted over in my heart.

I went immediately after church to the place where I had prayed the day before, and found the relief I had there received was but the earnest of a richer blessing. How shall I express what the Lord did for me, except by saying, that he made all his goodness to pass before me. I seemed to speak to him face to face, as a man conversing with his friend, except that my speech was only in tears of joy, and groanings which cannot be uttered. I could say, indeed, with Jacob, not "how dreadful," but how lovely, "is this place! This is none other, than the house of God."[1]

Four months I continued in my lodging. Some

1 Genesis 28:17.

few of the neighbors came to see me, but their visits were not very frequent; and, in general, I had but little intercourse, except with my God in Christ Jesus. It was he who made my solitude sweet, and the wilderness to bloom and blossom as the rose; and my meditation of him was so delightful, that if I had few other comforts, neither did I want any.

One day, however, towards the expiration of this period, I found myself in a state of desertion. That communion which I had so long been able to maintain with the Lord, was suddenly interrupted. I began to dislike my solitary situation, and to fear I should never be able to weather out the winter in so lonely a dwelling. Suddenly a thought struck me, which I shall not fear to call a suggestion of the good providence which had brought me to Huntingdon. A few months before, I had formed an acquaintance with the Rev. Mr. Unwin's family. His son, though he had heard that I rather declined society, than sought it, and though Mrs. Unwin herself dissuaded him from visiting me on that account, was yet so strongly inclined to it, that, notwithstanding all objections and arguments to the contrary, he one day engaged himself as we were coming out of church, after morning prayers, to drink tea with me that afternoon. To my inexpressible joy, I found him one whose notions of religion were spiritual and lively; one whom the Lord had been training up from his infancy for the service of the temple. We opened our hearts to each other at the first interview, and when we parted, I immediately retired to my chamber, and prayed the Lord, who had been the author, to be the guardian of our friendship, and to grant to it fervency and perpetuity, even unto death: and I doubt not that my gracious Father heard this prayer also.

The Sunday following I dined with him. That afternoon, while the rest of the family was withdrawn, I had much discourse with Mrs. Unwin. I am not at liberty to describe the pleasure I had in conversing with her, because she will be one of the first who will have the perusal of this narrative. Let it suffice to say, I found we had one faith, and had been baptized with the same baptism.

When I returned home, I gave thanks to God, who had so graciously answered my prayers, by bringing me into the society of Christians. She has since been a means in the hand of God of supporting, quickening, and strengthening me, in walk with him. It was long before I thought of any other connection with this family, than as a friend and neighbor. On the day, however, above mentioned, while I was revolving in my mind the nature of my situation, and beginning, for the first time, to find an irksomeness in such retirement, suddenly it occurred to me, that I might probably find a place in Mr. Unwin's family as a boarder. A young gentleman, who had lived with him as a pupil, was the day before gone to Cambridge. It appeared to me, at least, possible, than I might be allowed to succeed him. From the moment this thought struck me, such a tumult of anxious solicitude seized me, that for two or three days I could not divert my mind to any other subject. I blamed and condemned myself for want of submission to the Lord's will; but still the language of my mutinous and disobedient heart was, "Give me the blessing, or else I die."[1]

About the third evening after I had determined upon this measure, I, at length, made shift to fasten my thoughts upon a theme which had no manner of connection with it. While I was pursuing my meditations, Mr. Unwin and family quite out of sight, my attention was suddenly called home again by the words which had been continually playing in my mind, and were, at length, repeated with such importunity that I could not help regarding them: "The Lord God of truth will do this." I was effectually convinced, that they were not of my own production, and accordingly I received from them some assurance of success; but my unbelief and fearfulness robbed me of much of the comfort they were intended to convey; though I have since had many a blessed experience of the same kind, for which I can never be sufficiently thankful. I immediately began to negotiate the affair, and in a few days it was entirely concluded.

1  See Genesis 30:1.

I took possession of my new abode, Nov. 11, 1765. I have found it a place of rest prepared for me by God's own hand, where he has blessed me with a thousand mercies, and instances of his fatherly protection; and where he has given me abundant means of furtherance in the knowledge of our Lord Jesus, both by the study of his own word, and communion with his dear disciples. May nothing but death interrupt our union!

Peace be with the reader, through faith in our Lord Jesus Christ. Amen!

# Appendix No. I

*Extracts from* MR. COWPERS *Letters to his Friends and Relatives,* LADY HESKETH, *and* MRS. COWPER, *illustrative, chiefly, of the nature and effects of that remarkable change in his religious views and feelings, which he has described in the latter part of the preceding Memoir.*

*To Lady Hesketh, dated Huntingdon, July 1, 1765.*

Since the visit you were so kind as to pay me in the Temple, (the only time I ever saw you without pleasure) what have I not suffered? And since it has pleased God to restore me to the use of my reason, what have I not enjoyed? You know by experience, how pleasant it is to feel the first approaches of health after a fever; but, oh the fever of the brain! to feel the quenching of that fire, is indeed a blessing which I think it impossible to receive without the most consummate gratitude.

Terrible as this chastisement is, I acknowledge in it the hand of an infinite justice; nor is it at all more difficult for me to perceive in it the hand of an infinite mercy likewise, when I consider the effect it has had upon me. I am exceedingly thankful for it, and, without hypocrisy, esteem it the greatest blessing, next to life itself, I ever received from the divine bounty. I pray God that I may ever retain this sense of it, and then I am sure I shall continue to be as I am at present, really happy.

I write thus to you that you may not think me a forlorn and wretched creature; which you might be apt to do, considering my very distant removal from every friend I have in the world—a circumstance, which before this event befell me, would undoubtedly have made me so; but my affliction has taught me a road to happiness, which without it I should never have found; and I know, and have experience of it every day, that the mercy of God to him who believes himself the object of it, is more than sufficient to compensate for the loss of every other blessing.

You may now inform all those whom you think really interested in my welfare, that they have no need to be apprehensive on the score of my happiness at present. And you yourself will believe that my happiness is no dream, because I have told you the foundation on which it is built. What I have written would appear like enthusiasm to many, for we are apt to give that name to every warm affection of the mind in others, which we have not experienced in ourselves; but to you, who have so much to be thankful for, and a temper inclined to gratitude, it will not appear so.

———————

*To Lady Hesketh, dated Huntingdon, July 4, 1765.*

What could you think of my unaccountable behavior to you in that visit I mentioned in my last? I remember I neither spoke to you, nor looked at you. The solution of the mystery indeed followed soon after but at the same time, it must have been inexplicable. The uproar within was even then begun, and my silence was only the sulkiness of a thunder storm before it opens. I am glad, however, that the only instance, in which I knew not how to value your company, was, when I was not in my senses. It was the first of the kind, and I trust in God it will be the last.

How naturally does affliction make us Christians! and how impossible is it when all human help is vain, and the whole earth too poor and trifling to furnish us with one moment's peace, how impossible is it then to avoid looking at the Gospel! It gives me some concern, though at the same time it increases my gratitude, to reflect that a convert made in Bedlam is more likely to be a stumbling-block to others, than to advance their faith. But if it has that effect upon any, it is owing to their reasoning amiss, and drawing their conclusions from false premises. He who can ascribe an amendment of life and manners, and a reformation of the heart itself, to madness, is guilty of an absurdity, that in any other case would fasten the imputation of madness upon himself; for by so doing, he ascribes a reasonable effect to an unreasonable cause, and a positive effect to a negative. But when Christianity only is to be sacrificed, he that stabs deepest is always the wisest man. You, my dear Cousin, yourself, will be apt to think I carry the matter too far, and that, in the present warmth of my heart, I make too ample a concession in saying that I am *only now* a convert. You think I always believed, and I thought so too, but you were deceived, and so was I. I called myself indeed a Christian, but he who knows my heart, knows that I never did a right thing, nor abstained from a wrong one, because I was so. But if I did either, it was under the influence of some other motive. And it is such seeming Christians, such pretending believers, that do most mischief to the cause, and furnish the strongest arguments to support the infidelity of its enemies. Unless profession and conduct go together, the man's life is a lie, and the validity of what he professes itself is called in question. The difference between a Christian and an Unbeliever, would be so striking, if the treacherous allies of the Church would go over at once to the other side, that I am satisfied religion would be no loser by the bargain.

I reckon it one instance of the Providence that has attended me throughout this whole event, that instead of being delivered into the hands of one of the London physicians, who were so much nearer that I wonder I was not, I was carried to Doctor Cotton. I was not only treated by him with the greatest tenderness while I was ill, and attended with the utmost diligence, but when my reason was restored to me, and I had so much need of a religious friend to converse with, to whom I could open my mind upon the subject without reserve, I could hardly have found a fitter person for the purpose. My eagerness and anxiety to settle my opinions upon that long neglected point, made it necessary that while my mind was yet weak, and my spirits uncertain, I should have some assistance. The Doctor was as ready to administer relief to me in this article likewise, and as well qualified to do it, as in that which was more immediately his province. How many physicians would have thought this an irregular appetite, and symptom of vanishing madness! But if it were so, my friend was as mad as myself, and it is well for me that he was so.

My dear Cousin, you know not half the deliverances I have received; my brother is the only one in the family who does. My recovery is, indeed, a signal one, but a greater if possible went before it. My future life must express my thankfulness, for by words I cannot do it.

_____

*To Lady Hesketh, dated Huntingdon, Oct. 18, 1765.*

It was my earnest request, before I left St. Alban's, that wherever it might please Providence to dispose of me, I might meet with such an acquaintance as I find in Mrs. Unwin. How happy it is to believe with a steadfast assurance, that our petitions are heard even while we are making them—and how delightful to meet with a proof of it in the effectual and actual grant of them! Surely it is a gracious finishing given to those means, which the Almighty has been pleased to make use of for my conversion—after having been deservedly rendered unfit for any society, to be again qualified for it, and admitted at once into the fellowship of those, whom God regards as the excellent of the earth, and whom, in the emphatical language of Scripture, he preserves as the apple of his eye, is a blessing, which carries with it the stamp and visible superscription of divine bounty—a grace unlimited as undeserved; and, like its glorious Author, free in its course, and blessed in its operation!

My dear Cousin! health and happiness, and above all, the favor of our great and gracious Lord attend you! While we seek it in spirit and in truth, we are infinitely more secure of it than of the next breath we expect to draw. Heaven and earth have their destined periods; ten thousand worlds will vanish at the consummation of all things; but the Word of God standeth fast, and they who trust in him shall never be confounded.

---

*To Lady Hesketh, dated Huntingdon, March 6, 1766.*

I have for some time past imputed your silence to the cause which you yourself assign for it, *viz.* to my change of situation; and was even sagacious enough to account for the frequency of your letters to me, while I lived alone, from your attention to me in a state of such solitude as seemed to make it an act of particular charity to write to me. I bless God for it, I was happy even then; solitude has nothing gloomy in it, if the soul points upwards. St. Paul tells his Hebrew converts, "Ye are come (already come) to Mount Sion, to an innumerable company of angels, to the general assembly of the first-born, which are written in heaven, and to Jesus the mediator of the new covenant."[1] When this is the case, as surely it was with them, or the Spirit of Truth had never spoken it, there is an end of the melancholy and dullness of a solitary life at once. You will not suspect me, my dear Cousin, of a design to understand this passage literally. But this however it certainly means, that a lively faith is able to anticipate, in some measure, the joys of that heavenly society, which the soul shall actually possess hereafter.

1 Hebrews 12:22, 23, 24.

Since I have changed my situation, I have found still greater cause of thanksgiving to the Father of all mercies. The family with whom I live are Christians, and it has pleased the Almighty to bring me to the knowledge of them, that I may want no means of improvement in that temper and conduct, which he is pleased to require in all his servants.

My dear Cousin! one half of the Christian world would call this madness, fanaticism, and folly: but are not these things warranted by the Word of God, not only in the passages I have cited, but in many others? If we have no communion with God here, surely we can expect none hereafter. A faith that does not place our conversation in heaven, that does not warm the heart, and purify it too, that does not, in short, govern our thought, word, and deed, is no faith; nor will it obtain for us any spiritual blessing here or hereafter. Let us see, therefore, my dear Cousin, that we do not deceive ourselves in a matter of such infinite moment. The world will be ever telling us, that we are good enough, and the same world will vilify us behind our backs. But it is not the world which tries the heart; that is the prerogative of God alone.

---

*To Mrs. Cowper, dated Huntingdon, March 11, 1766.*

I am much obliged to you for Pearsall's Meditations, especially as it furnishes me with an

occasion of writing to you, which is all I have waited
for. My friends must excuse me, if I write to none
but those, who lay it fairly in my way to do so. The
inference I am apt to draw from their silence is, that
they wish *me* to be silent too.

• • • • •

Your brother Martin (the Rev. Mr. Madan) has
been very kind to me, having wrote to me twice in
a style, which, though it once was irksome to me, to
say the least, I now know how to value. I pray God
to forgive me the many light things I have both said
and thought of him and his labors. Hereafter I shall
consider him as a burning and a shining light, and
as one of those who, having turned many to righteousness, shall shine hereafter as the stars for ever
and ever.

So much for the state of my heart; as to my spirits I am cheerful and happy, and having peace with
God, have peace within myself. For the continuance
of this blessing, I trust to Him who gives it; and they
who trust in Him shall never be confounded.

———————

*Letter to Mrs. Cowper, dated April 4, 1766.*

I agree with you that letters are not essential to
friendship, but they seem to be a natural fruit of it,
when they are the only intercourse that can be had.
And a friendship producing no sensible effects is so

like indifference, that the appearance may easily deceive even an acute discerner. I retract, however, all that I said in my last upon this subject, having reason to suspect that it proceeded from a principle which I would discourage in myself upon all occasions, even a pride that felt itself hurt upon a mere suspicion of neglect. I have so much cause for humility, and so much need of it too, and every little sneaking resentment is such an enemy to it, that I hope I shall never give quarter to any thing that appears in the shape of sullenness or self-consequence hereafter. Alas! if my best friend, who laid down his life for me, were to remember all the instances, in which I have neglected him, and to plead them against me in judgment, where should I hide my guilty head in the day of recompense? I will pray, therefore, for blessings upon my friends, even though they cease to be so, and upon my enemies though they continue such. The deceitfulness of the natural heart is inconceivable: I know well that I passed upon my friends for a person at least religiously inclined, if not actually religious, and what is more wonderful, I thought myself a Christian, when I had no faith in Christ, when I saw no beauty in him, that I should desire him, in short when I had neither faith nor love, nor any Christian grace whatever, but a thousand seeds of rebellion instead, ever more springing up in enmity against him. But blessed be God, even the God who is become my salvation. The hail of affliction, and rebuke for sin, has swept away the refuge of lies. It pleased the Almighty, in great mercy, to set all my misdeeds before me. At length, the storm being past, a quiet and peaceful serenity of soul succeeded, such as ever attends the gift of lively faith in the all-sufficient atonement, and the sweet sense of mercy and pardon purchased by the blood of Christ. Thus did he break me, and bind me up; thus did he wound me, and his hands made me whole. My dear Cousin; I make no apology for entertaining you with the history of my conversion, because I know you to be a Christian in the sterling import of the appellation. This is, however, but a very summary account of the matter, neither would a letter contain the astonishing particulars of it. If we ever meet again in this world, I will relate them to you by word of mouth; if not, they will serve for the subject of a conference in the next, where I doubt not I shall remember and record them with a gratitude better suited to the subject.

———————

*Letter to Mrs. Cowper, dated Sept. 3, 1766.*

You are so kind as to inquire after my health, for which reason I must tell you, what otherwise would not be worth mentioning, that I have lately been just enough indisposed to convince me, that not only human life in general, but mine in particular, hangs by a slender thread. I am stout enough in appearance, yet a little illness demolishes me. I have had a severe shake, and the building is not so firm as it was. But I bless God for it with all my heart. If the inner man be but strengthened day by day, as I hope, under the renewing influences of the Holy Ghost, it will be, no matter how soon the outward is dissolved. He who has in a manner raised me from the dead, in a literal sense, has given me the grace, I trust, to be ready at the shortest notice to surrender up to him that life, which I have twice received from him. Whether I live or die, I desire it may be to His Glory, and it must be to my happiness.—I thank God that I have those amongst my kindred to whom I can write without reserve my sentiments upon this subject, as I do to you. A letter upon any other subject is more insipid to me than ever my task was, when a school-boy; and I say not this in vain glory, God forbid! but to show you what the Almighty, whose name I am unworthy to mention, has done for me, the chief of sinners. Once he was a terror to me, and his service, oh what a weariness it was! Now I can say I love him and his holy name, and am never so happy as when I speak of his mercies to me.

---

*Letter to Mrs. Cowper, dated Oct. 20, 1766.*

That Jesus is a *present* Saviour from the guilt of sin by his most precious blood, and from the power of it by his Spirit; that corrupt and wretched in ourselves, in Him, and in Him only, we are complete; that being united to Jesus by a lively faith, we have a solid and eternal interest in his obedience and sufferings, to justify us before the face of our heavenly Father, and that all this inestimable treasure, the earnest of which is in grace, and its consummation in glory, is given, freely *given* to us of God; in short, that he hath opened the kingdom of heaven to *all believers*. These are the Truths, which, by the grace of God, shall ever be dearer to me than life itself; shall ever be placed next my heart as the throne whereon the Saviour himself shall sit, to sway all its motions, and reduce that world of iniquity and rebellion to a state of filial and affectionate obedience to the will of the Most Holy.

These, my dear Cousin, are the truths to which by nature we are enemies—they debase the sinner, and exalt the Saviour, to a degree which the pride of our hearts (till Almighty grace subdues them) is determined never to allow. May the Almighty reveal his Son in our hearts continually more and more, and teach us to increase in love towards him continually, for having given us the unspeakable riches of Christ.

# Appendix No. II

*Extracts from a* "REVIEW *of the third Volume of* MR. HAYLEY'S *Life and Posthumous Writings of* COWPER," *which appeared in the Christian Observer for the year 1805; containing Remarks on the alleged connection between his mental derangement and his religious experience, and including brief sketch of his history, from the period at which the preceding Memoir concludes, to the time of his death.*

While he, (MR. COWPER) was yet under Dr. Cotton's roof, his religious views underwent a very considerable revolution.—We have, on a former occasion, expressed our opinion, an opinion grounded on the facts of the case, that this change, so far from having either produced, or contributed to increase his unhappy malady, as some contemporary critics have affirmed, had a most salutary influence on his mind.[1] And this opinion seems to derive the most satisfactory confirmation from the letters now under review.

. . . Surely no man, after reading these extracts, will venture to affirm that Cowper's religion, or, if they please, his methodism, for many choose to give it that name, was the cause of his insanity, or even contributed to its production. That unhappy malady was unquestionably constitutional, and it was so far from having been aggravated at this time by religious feeling, that to his religion may be ascribed, under God, the lucid interval of many years which followed what he himself calls, and we think justly, his *conversion*. His own testimony to this point, as it appears in these confidential letters, is express and unequivocal; and it goes to prove, that what had been chiefly instrumental in producing the happy state of mind which he enjoyed during his residence at Huntingdon, as well as during the first part of his stay at Olney, was the new view which he had been led to take of religion. Our readers, we trust, will excuse our dwelling on this subject so long. We feel solicitous to rescue real Christianity, such Christianity as was that of Cowper at the period to which we allude, from the imputation of melancholy, enthusiasm,

---

1 His first illness preceded the change to which we allude, and could not, therefore, be the effect of that change. (*Original footnote*)

or folly. Are these, we would ask, the proper terms by which the dispositions manifested in the above quotations should be designated? Instead of a religion of gloom and perturbation and weakness, do we not there see a religion which enlivens, while it calms and strengthens the mind, and in the place of dark despondency and feverish irritation, fills it with serenity and peace and heavenly consolation; a religion which, placing in its true light the comparative importance of temporal and eternal things, rectifies the corrupt bias that leads us too generally to prefer the former to the latter; a religion which raises the human aim to objects worthy of our best ambition, and gives to the human character a dignity and elevation suited to the relation wherein we stand to God and to Christ, as well as to the hope of heavenly glory which a sense of the divine favor naturally tends to inspire? Who would not be content to be found, at the coming of our Lord, in that frame of mind in which these Letters represent Cowper to have lived at the period of which we speak? Behold in him a lively example of that righteousness, peace, and joy in the Holy Ghost, which constitute the kingdom of God in the hearts of men; of that faith which overcomes the world, and purifies the heart, and which realizing the presence, the providence, the wisdom, and the goodness of the Almighty, in all his dispensations, however trying to flesh and blood, produces a tranquil submission to the will of God, and a cheerful acquiescence in his appointments; of that deadness to the world and to sin; of that poverty of spirit; and of that fervent love to God and man, which are the distinguishing features in the character of a real Christian. It is worthy of notice that, under the influence of this benign religion, even his insanity, which in ordinary cases would have formed a subject of the most painful recollection, is regarded with complacency. It is spoken of by him not only with calmness and composure, but even with expressions of the most fervent gratitude, as the happy instrument of making him acquainted with God and with his own heart.[1] Could a stronger proof than this be given of the soundness and sobriety of his religious views, and of their tendency to subdue improper feelings, and to bring every thought into subjection to the law of Christ?

. . . We have already shown that the first attack of morbid melancholy, which Cowper experienced, was owing in no degree to his religion. The malady was unquestionably constitutional. His bodily frame was naturally nervous and irritable, and his mind, even in his boyish days, peculiarly timid. He was early assaulted, as he himself states, with

---

1  This circumstance of itself, unless it be asserted that Cowper was still under the influence of mental derangement, completely disproves what has been affirmed respecting the effect which religion had in producing his malady. *(Original footnote)*

"gloomy thoughts led on by spleen." And this natural propensity was greatly aggravated by a disap-
pointment in love; an union with the object of his
attachment having been prevented by the friends
of both parties on prudential grounds. At length,
when it became necessary for him to enter on his
office in the House of Lords, his terror and agitation
were so violent as to deprive him of his reason; and
he sunk into a state of the severest mental depression. This grievous calamity continued with little or
no abatement, from December 1763, to July 1764.
He then began, under the kind care of Dr. Cotton,
to emerge from the depth of his despondency. But
the circumstance which was chiefly instrumental in
restoring him to soundness of mind was, without
doubt, the new view which he had been led to take
of religion during his residence with Dr. Cotton.

Cowper, though in his youth he professed a
belief in revelation, yet had felt nothing, according
to his own acknowledgement, of the practical influence of Christianity. He called himself a Christian,
and in his conduct was far more decorous than the
generality of his youthful associates: yet he affirms
that, previous to the change of sentiment of which
we now speak, he had never abstained from a bad
action, or performed a good one, from religious
motives, or because he was a Christian. It was not
possible for any man to open his Bible, and read
it with an earnest desire to know the will of God,

without discovering that such a state of mind was there condemned, in terms the most awful and affecting. That this discovery, unaccompanied by a soothing sense of the mercy and loving-kindness of God, is calculated to aggravate, and even to create, mental depression, will readily be admitted: we are far, therefore, from saying that the strong impression made on the mind of Cowper of his sinfulness, guilt, and danger, did in no way add to his disquiet. It probably did. But then this was an effect no more to be deplored, than the pain attending some course of medicine, or some operation in surgery, which is to issue in relieving the patient from a threatened mortification, and restoring him to perfect health.—Without such a view of our guilt and danger as is attended with painful emotions, without deep sorrow and contrition on account of our sins, it is evident that there can be no due preparation for the grace of the Gospel, and that no effectual cure can be wrought in the soul. "Except ye repent, ye shall all likewise perish."[1] But what is it to repent? Is it not to feel that we are *miserable* sinners" in whom "there is *no* health?" Is it not that the remembrance of our sins has become *grievous* to us, and "the burden of them *intolerable?*" Is it not to deplore our past transgressions, and earnestly to seek deliverance from them; as well as from future punishment? The morbid state of Cowper's mind,

1 Luke 13:3.

may, without doubt, at this period, have given to his remorse of conscience too much of the color of despair. But let no man, therefore, infer that the depth of penitential sorrow, and the awful dread of the just judgments of God, which Cowper experienced, were not salutary feelings. Such feelings, in kind, though not in degree, are essential to salvation. They are the solid ground-work of true peace and consolation. To a mind which is a total stranger to this godly sorrow, the Gospel of Christ can possess but comparatively feeble attractions: for its grand object is to deliver man from the guilt and power of sin, and from the fear of divine wrath, and to introduce him to the enjoyment of that heavenly peace which arises from the promises of forgiveness, of reconciliation with God, of grace here, and of glory hereafter.

It pleased God that Cowper should not long remain under the influence of those terrors, which a view of the violated obligations and extensive demands of the divine law had excited. He was judiciously directed to the Bible, though it had been in some measure the cause of his distress, as the only source of true consolation. And in that blessed book he found the relief which he sought. The third chapter of St. Paul's epistle to the Romans, by which his attention might possibly have been drawn to the sins of his heart and life, was made the means of conveying to him, in the first instance, such a view of the grace of Christ as dissipated his terrors, and inspired him with a lively trust and confidence in the mercy of God.[1] Thus, to use the words of his biographer, "were his ideas of religion changed from the gloom of terror and despair; to the luster of comfort and delight."

. . . His health now rapidly mended, and in June, 1765, he had so far recovered, that it was no longer thought necessary that he should continue under the roof of Dr. Cotton; and he took up his abode at Huntingdon. The happy state of mind which he enjoyed at this time, and which seems to have continued without interruption, during the whole of his stay at Huntingdon, as well as during the first part of his residence at Olney, to which place he removed with Mrs. Unwin, in 1768, has been noticed in our last number. In 1773, however, his malady returned, and he sunk into a state of the blackest despondency, from which he did not begin to recover till the year 1778; and it was two years later before his mind was sufficiently restored to allow of his engaging in literary composition.

That the disorder which again visited Cowper was deeply rooted in his constitution, has already appeared; and to this cause we must principally ascribe its recurrence. For a person in whom there existed so strong a tendency towards derangement,

1 The particular passage which excited these feelings, was Romans 3:24–26. (*Original footnote*)

it must, however, be fairly admitted, that the mode in which he passed his life at Olney, previous to this attack, was not judiciously contrived. He should have had some well chosen occupation to engage his mind; instead of which, a great part of his days were spent in idleness; and the only fruits which remain of the labors of five years are a few hymns and familiar letters. That a considerable portion of his time was given to devotional exercises must be acknowledged: but that devotion which does not issue in action partakes too much of the religion of the cloister, to have the effect of keeping the mind long in a healthy state. The right use of time is a very important division of Christian duty; and here, we cannot help thinking that Cowper failed. Devotional exercises, instead of being used to prepare and strengthen the mind for the active duties of life, were allowed, in a great measure, to usurp their place; and not only was the opportunity thus lost of benefiting mankind, by labors which would probably have proved their own reward, even in the peace and satisfaction they imparted to his own bosom; but the natural timidity and feminine softness of his character must have been increased, by his almost total seclusion from the world. . . .

. . . The death of his brother, whom he most tenderly loved, and whose loss he severely felt, may possibly have contributed to depress his spirits at this period. However that may be, he was a second time overwhelmed with a gloom which rendered five or six years of his life a perfect blank. On his recovery from this melancholy state, his friends, who had probably regarded his want of some regular employment as one of the predisposing causes of his illness, prevailed with him to turn his thoughts to writing. We now see him regularly occupied; and the beneficial effect which this circumstance had on his mind sufficiently appears, both from the Poems which he first published, and from the letters which, while employed in composing them, he addressed to his friends. These show, that while he was moderately and usefully occupied, while he had an object in view which served to keep his mind from preying on itself, he enjoyed a sufficient share of mental quiet and satisfaction. Nor were these blessings obtained by any undue sacrifice of devotional feeling, or religious meditation. The poems, and many of the letters, which he then wrote, prove that religion still occupied the chief place in his thoughts. They prove also the scriptural soundness, the cheering tendency, the purifying and elevating effect, of those views of Christianity which Cowper had embraced: nor do we hesitate in giving it as our opinion, that the labors of that period of his life of which we speak, will long continue to be the delight and admiration, not only of all who have a taste for poetic excellence, but of all who have a cordial relish for divine truth, the effects and triumphs of which he has so beautifully described. They manifest throughout the genuine spirit of Christianity; and carry with them, to the mind of a Christian, intrinsic evidence, that they flowed from a heart which felt the full force of the truths that he taught. Let one instance serve to exemplify this opinion.

> Since the dear hour that brought me to thy foot,
> And cut up all my follies by the root,
> I never trusted in an arm but thine,
> Nor hoped but in thy righteousness divine;
> My prayers and alms, imperfect and defiled,
> Were but the feeble efforts of a child,
> Howe'er performed, it was their brightest part,
> That they proceeded from a grateful heart;
> Cleansed in thine own all purifying blood,
> Forgive their evil and accept their good:
> I cast them at thy feet, my only plea
> Is what it was, dependence upon thee:
> While struggling in the vale of tears below,
> That never failed, nor shall it fail me now.

But after "The Task" was published, Cowper seems to have passed from the error of doing *nothing* to that of doing *too much*. The translation of Homer was a vast undertaking, and could not fail to oppress his tender spirits. It proved a drudgery of many years continuance, denying him those intervals of leisure which were necessary to a mind of so peculiar a texture, and which a task of more moderate dimensions would have afforded.

It may be objected to what is said above, that though Cowper now entered into a more cheerful kind of society than he had before enjoyed, his malady returned after a time in its full strength. But it should be recollected, that in this more cheerful circle, there was nothing which had a tendency to produce or cherish what he principally needed— that fixed and settled serenity of soul which is founded on a sense of the favor of the Almighty; in other words, the peace of God in his heart. His new acquaintance were sprightly, amiable, and polished; but as to religion, there was among them, it is to be feared, the silence and vacuity of death. Well informed as was the mind of Cowper on that great subject, it could have found nothing on which to stay itself in the conversation of such persons. On the contrary, he must often have seen occasion for self-reproach in attachments and enjoyments, from which religion was almost wholly excluded. The attentions however of these persons could not but prove gratifying to him, and in concurrence with their power of ministering to his amusement, by the liveliness of their conversation, would be likely to have an imposing effect on his mind; while the sweetness of his nature would incline him to give them in return such pleasures as he knew would be acceptable. Thus were his thoughts too much diverted from religious subjects: so that admitting that these worldly associations did not taint his mind with a bad principle, which we believe they did not, yet they could not fail to lower the tone of his piety, and to deaden the warmth of his spiritual affections. They might often make him forget himself; but they would not lead him to God.[1] This kind of society, therefore, afforded no remedy likely to counteract that distempered tendency of mind with which he seems to have been born.

It is painful to advert to the gradual disappearance of religion from the letters of Cowper. But we do it for the purpose of making a remark or two which may not be without their use. His abstinence from religious topics seems to have kept pace with his growing fame, and the increase of

1 How strikingly is that truth, which it is our object to enforce, illustrated by Cowper himself in the following lines, the exquisite beauty of which is above all praise.

> Thou art the source and centre of all minds,
> Their only point of rest, Eternal Word!
> From thee departing, they are lost, and rove
> At random, without honour, hope, or peace.
> From thee is all that soothes the life of man,
> His high endeavor, and his glad success,
> His strength to suffer, and his will to serve.
> But oh! thou bounteous Giver of all good,
> Thou art of all thy gifts thyself the crown!
> Give what thou canst, without thee we are poor;
> And with thee rich, take what thou wilt away.
> *(Original footnote)*

his worldly friendships. The warmth of his piety, if we may judge from his two volumes of poetry, had suffered no material abatement, at the time of their composition; and this conclusion is greatly strengthened by the letters now under our review. But subsequent to the year 1785, when his productions had gained him so great an accession of literary fame, as served to draw around him a host of professed admirers, we see the case greatly altered. No man has pointed out more forcibly than Cowper himself, the pernicious influence of human applause, and of that vanity which it feeds and cherishes. That he was susceptible of their influence, and not sufficiently on his guard against them, the volume before us affords many proofs. Indeed, he states himself to have been a strange compound of ambition and shyness. As to worldly friendships, their nature and tendency are so clearly pointed out in the Word of God, that we should have had great cause to wonder, had any one who permitted himself to form them experienced none of their prejudicial effects.

The main employment of Cowper's late years, the translation of Homer, was little suited to correct the religious disadvantages under which he labored. On the contrary, it probably tended to increase them, by not only diverting his mind from those subjects which alone could be instrumental in procuring the peace and composure of which he stood in need; but by habitually directing his thoughts to objects which required the correcting influence of religion to prevent their producing positive injury.

The paralytic seizure which Mrs. Unwin experienced, in 1792, seems to have given a shock to Cowper's mind, from which it never recovered. His melancholy and dejection gradually increased, being doubtless accelerated in their progress by the constant view of his helpless and silent companion, till in the year 1794, his tremendous malady returned with all its force, and continued, with a few occasional glimpses of mental sanity, till his death in 1800.

The effect of all the circumstances which we have mentioned was, doubtless, aggravated by the pecuniary embarrassments which he began to feel during a few of the years which preceded his last attack. From these he was at length relieved by the pension of 300*l.* a year, granted to him by his Majesty; but it came too late to have much effect in removing the depression which had unhappily begun to overwhelm his faculties. On the whole, it appears, that considering the circumstance of Cowper's predisposition to insanity, his lot, after he left Dr. Cotton, was not cast in the most favorable situation for preventing a relapse. Indeed it may fairly be doubted, whether in any situation, or under any management, this melancholy event could have been averted.

We have been surprised to hear some persons, notwithstanding their having read the work which is now under review, still assigning Methodism as the cause of Cowper's derangement. But if this were the true cause, a methodistical taint must have been communicated to him before he was born: for his malady was evidently interwoven in his constitution, and was coeval with his existence. Towards the latter part of his stay at Weston, he seemed to be placed in circumstances highly favorable to his release from the gloom which haunted him. After Mrs. Unwin's seizure, a relation of the name of Johnson came to reside with him; a young man of affectionate manners, who waited on him like a child, read to him, transcribed for him, and did every thing that youth and gaiety could perform to enliven his situation. His cousin, Lady Hesketh, too, made one of his family; a person of fine understanding, great powers of entertainment, and uncommon sweetness of disposition; who devoted herself to the care of Cowper, suffered him to want no earthly comfort, watched over him with the affection of a sister, and possessed, as did Mr. (now Dr.) Johnson, the power of engaging his attention to a degree that was evidently beneficial to his health and spirits. By the company of these two amiable and well-educated friends, a new experiment was made on Cowper. He loved them, and seemed to feel, that by their society the comforts of his situation were greatly increased. They practiced, for some time with success, the art of exhilarating his mind, without, at the same time, attempting, or wishing, to prevent him from attending to subjects of everlasting importance. But all failed. They stayed longer than the sunshine which they brought with them continued. They stayed, till they became witnesses of the permanent triumph which his constitutional malady obtained over all their kind endeavors to gladden the remainder of his days.

[See Christian Observer, 1805; pp. 103–106; and pp. 165–170]

# Appendix No. III

*Observations on the Sin of* Suicide, *and on the futility of those false reasonings by which its vindication has sometimes been attempted.*

*Extract from one of Mr. Cowper's letters to the Rev. William Unwin, dated July 12, 1784.*

I have not yet read the last Review, but dipping into it, I accidentally fell upon their account of Hume's Essay on Suicide. I am glad that they have liberality enough to condemn the licentiousness of an author whom they so much admire. I say liberality, for there is as much bigotry in the world to that man's errors, as there is in the hearts of some sectaries to their peculiar modes and tenets. He is the pope of thousands, as blind and as presumptuous as himself. God certainly infatuates those who will not see. It were otherwise impossible that a man, naturally shrewd and sensible, and whose understanding has had all the advantages of constant exercise and cultivation, could have satisfied himself, or have hoped to satisfy others, with such palpable sophistry as has not even the grace of fallacy to recommend it. His silly assertion, that because it would be no sin to divert the course of the Danube, therefore it is none to let out a few ounces of blood from an artery, would justify not suicide only, but homicide also. For the lives of ten thousand men are of less consequence to their country, than the course of that river to the legions through which it flows. Population would soon make society amends for the loss of her ten thousand members, but the loss of the Danube would be felt by all the millions that dwell upon its banks, to all generations. But the life of a man, and the water of a river, can never come into competition with each other, in point of value, unless in the estimation of an unprincipled philosopher.

———————

*Extracts from "Two Discourses on the Guilt, Folly, and Sources of Suicide," preached and published at New York, in the year 1805, by Samuel Miller, D.D.*

There have been some who professed to believe that, although no man has a right to take away the life of *another*, yet every man has a right to dispose of *his own* life. In opposition to these, it is my purpose to show, that suicide is a sin against God—against human nature—against, our fellow men—and against all our interests and hopes beyond the grave.

1. To destroy our own lives, is a *sin against God.* That God is the author of our existence; that he sent us into the world; and that our time and talents, as well as our persons, are his property, are self-evident propositions, which none but an atheist will deny. To suppose that rational and moral creatures, endowed with such capacities, and formed for such activity, could have come into existence by accident, or without any specific destination, is too unreasonable for credulity itself to admit. But if there be a God who made us, who has a right to our services, and whose Providence extends to all his creatures and all their actions, then there is an *end* for which we were made, a *task* which we are bound to accomplish, a *term of service* which it is our duty to fulfill; and, of course, he alone who placed us here, has a right to decide when this task is done, to judge when this term of service ought to close, and, in a word, to dispose of the life and the talents which his power has bestowed.

This is the representation which the Scriptures every where give of human life. They speak of it a *term* assigned, a *course* marked out, a *race set before us.* Hence the pious *Job* asks, "Is there not an appointed time to man upon earth? Are not his days also like the days of an hireling?"[1] And in the spirit

1 Job 7:1.

of the principle which this interrogation implies, he resolves, "All the days of my appointed time will I wait till my change come."[1] The same lesson is taught by the apostle Paul, when he exhorts, "Let us run with patience the race that is set before us";[2] when he expresses an earnest desire to "finish his course with joy"; and when, toward the close of life, he exclaims in holy triumph, "I have finished my course, I have kept the faith."[3] Such is the language in which the inspired writers speak of the life of man; a language which plainly teaches us that, we are not at liberty to dispose of our own lives,[4] or to determine the period of our continuance in the world; but that we are to be patient and active as long as God is pleased to retain us in the present state, and

1 Job 14:14.

2 Hebrews 12:1.

3 2 Timothy 4:7.

4 It will, perhaps, be said, that this reasoning, if admitted, would prove too much; for if no man have a right to dispose of his own life; and if all the legitimate authority of civil government over individuals be founded in compact, then no government can have a right to take away life, even for the most atrocious crimes; because no individual can, by any act of his own, either express or implied, convey to a community a right which he does not himself possess. But this objection proceeds upon an erroneous principle. The right of civil government to take away life, in certain cases, arises not from compact, but from the will of God, explicitly revealed in his Word. We may even go further. Men would have no right to take away the lives of inferior animals, had there not been an express grant of the Creator for this purpose. *(Original footnote)*

to wait his pleasure for the period of our dismission. To take into our own hands the decision of this question, to abandon, without leave, the station in which we are placed, is the most unequivocal rebellion against God; the most direct opposition to his Providence; a presumptuous attempt to escape from his control; and an ignoble breach of fidelity to a rightful sovereign.

Some of the advocates of this crime have contended, that as God is a benevolent Being, who delights in the happiness of his creatures, he cannot be supposed to regard with displeasure one who lays down his life when he ceases to enjoy it. But if this position be admitted, then it will follow, that every man is at liberty to pursue his own happiness in whatever way he chooses, or, which is the same thing, that no act is displeasing to God, or a crime, which the agent commits with a view of promoting his own happiness. A doctrine which, if conceded, would lead to the justification of the most atrocious crimes; would destroy the firmest principles of moral obligation; and render the caprice of man, instead of the Divine law; the ultimate rule of action.

2. Suicide is a *sin against human nature*. If there be a crime that may be called *unnatural*, this is emphatically that crime. It offers violence to the principle of self-preservation, which is innate and universal. It an outrage on the dignity of those

faculties with which the Author of nature has endowed us; and it is not less inconsistent with the virtues of fortitude and self-command, which so highly exalt and adorn the human character.

The fear of death is one of the strongest principles that dwells in the bosom of man. But why should this principle operate not only more generally and strongly in human beings than in the other animals, but almost exclusively in the former? It is difficult to assign any other reason for this fact, than that the all-wise Creator intended it as a barrier against the crime which we are considering; a crime which the brutal tribes have neither temptation nor ability to commit; but against which man, depraved, afflicted, and covered with evil, requires to be guarded by restraints of the most powerful kind. He then, who breaks through these restraints, who surmounts that abhorrence of self-destruction which the Author of nature hath so closely interwoven with every fiber of our constitution, is as great a monster in morals as an atheist in religion, or as the most hideous assemblage in animal nature.

But suicide is not only repugnant to every genuine feeling of human nature; it also offers insult to every just principle of human dignity. I know that the advocates of suicide are, in general, the most loquacious assertors of the *dignity of man*. This is the idol which they profess to worship, and contending for its honors they consider as their greatest merit.

But does it comport with the dignity of our nature to act the part of cowards, poltroons, and deserters? Have fortitude, patience, and self-command ceased to be virtues? Putting moral and religious obligation out of the question, is it not more honorable for a rational being to bear afflictions with firmness, to meet misfortunes with magnanimity, and to surmount difficulties with triumph, than to sink under their pressure, or to fly from the conflict?

The outrage which this crime offers to the noble faculties with which the Creator has endowed us, also deserves our serious consideration. If the soul of man were less important, if his faculties were less dignified, the extinction of life would be an event comparatively trivial; the violence which it does to our nature would be of smaller account. But voluntarily to destroy a life, which is connected with the exercise of such exalted powers; wantonly to cut off a moral agent, so capable of activity and usefulness; to extinguish talents so rich, various, and productive; is offering a violence to human nature, as degrading as it is criminal. Nor is this reasoning invalidated by contending, as some advocates of suicide have done, that to destroy this mortal life is liberating these noble faculties from a species of imprisonment, and transferring them to a more enlarged and useful sphere of action. How do they learn this? The immortality of the soul, and a future state of bliss or suffering, are fully ascertained by Revelation only: a Revelation which, while it unfolds to our view another world, solemnly forbids us to precipitate ourselves by suicide into its awful realities.

3. Suicide is a *sin against society*. The benevolent Creator, who placed us in this world, has bound us to our fellow men, by many strong and interesting relations. These differ in number and in kind, according to circumstances; but they exist in all cases, and under all varieties of condition. It is a dictate of nature, as well as a doctrine of Revelation, that *no man liveth to himself, and no man dieth to himself.*

The community has just claims upon *all* its members, from the highest to the lowest; and to violate these claims, or to abandon the duties which they involve, is a criminal desertion, a fraud practiced upon our species, an injury, the extent of which it is impossible to calculate, but which we have reason to believe is, in most cases, serious and lasting. Nor let any one plead that his case is peculiar, and that society can lose but little by the destruction of a single life: for if one individual, because he feels the inclination, has a right to take away his own life, then every other individual who feels a similar inclination has the same right; and if every one were to think and act accordingly, into what a field of blood would our world be converted! what darkness and mourning would cover the face of society!

what distrust, anxiety, and consternation would reign in every family, and torture every bosom!

But we may go further. Besides the injury done to society in general, he who destroys his own life seldom fails to inflict the deepest wounds upon all who stand more immediately related to him in domestic and social life. Say, miserable man! who art contemplating the crime of self-murder, hast thou no parent, the evening of whose days, by this crime, would be embittered, or whose grey hairs would be brought down with sorrow to the grave? Hast thou no amiable partner of thy life, who would be precipitated by this step into the deepest affliction? Hast thou no tender babes, who by thy desertion would be left fatherless, and exposed to all the dangers of an unpitying world? Hast thou no brethren or sisters to share in the grief, and the disgrace of thine unworthy conduct? Are there no friends who love thee, who would weep over thy folly and sin, and feel themselves wounded by thy fall? In short, would the execution of thy wicked purpose disturb the peace of no family? torture no bosom of sensibility and kindness? defraud no creditor? plunge no friend into difficulty? rob no fellow creature of advantage or enjoyment? Ah! if the evil terminated in thine own person, though still a crime, it would be comparatively small. But the consequences of such a step would probably extend beyond thy conception, and last longer than thy memory. Stay then!

guilty man! stay thy murderous hand! Extinguish not the happiness and the hopes of a family, it may be, of many families! Forbear, O forbear to inflict wounds which no time can heal, and which may tempt survivors to wish that thou hadst never been born.

Let no one say, that he is useless in the world; that his life is of no value, either to his relatives, or to mankind; and, therefore, that he does no injury by taking it away. If any man be really useless, it is his disgrace and his sin; and to think of justifying one crime by pleading that he has committed a previous one, is as wretched logic as it is detestable morality. But the degree of our usefulness in society is a question concerning which, as we are not competent to judge, so we are not at liberty to decide for ourselves. The victim of depression and melancholy may sometimes think himself an unprofitable member of the community, a mere cumberer of the ground, when his services are really substantial and important. And even admitting that he is, at present, so afflicted, so infirm, so vicious, so degraded, or so unfavorably situated in any respect, as to be entirely useless, has he lost every capacity of being otherwise in time to come? Or, if this capacity be now lost, is every possibility of recovering it certainly precluded? May not his infirmities be hereafter removed? the clouds which hang over him be dissipated? his vices be repented of and abandoned?

his reputation be restored? and his means of use-fulness become, if not great and extensive, at least important in a moderate sphere? If these things be duly considered, it will be manifest that there is not an individual breathing who can, with propriety, plead in defense of despair and suicide, that he is useless; as there is certainly no individual, on this side the grave, whose life either is not, or might not be, of some value to mankind.

It may be demonstrated then, that suicide is gen-erally prompted by the most sordid and unworthy selfishness. It is a crime which sacrifices every thing on the altar of individual feeling. It is a practice which reverses all the doctrines of social benevo-lence, and sets up as a principle of action the detest-able maxim, that private caprice and private enjoy-ment are to be regarded as more worthy objects of pursuit than public happiness. It is a crime, there-fore, of which even the atheist, on his own princi-ples, ought to be ashamed, but which the Christian should regard with peculiar abhorrence.

4. Once more; suicide *is solemnly forbidden by all our interests and hopes beyond the grave.*

It is common to see announced, in our vehicles of public intelligence, that such an one, in a melan-choly hour, "put an end to his own *existence.*" It were well for those who live and die in rebellion against God, if death were really the termination of their existence; for hideous as is the thought of sinking into the gulf of annihilation, even this gulf would be preferable to the abyss of the damned. But alas! wretched as this hope is, it is cherished in vain. The infidel, indeed, will tell me that death is nothing; that it is only "diverting from its ordinary channel a portion of that red fluid" which appears necessary to the vital functions; that in destroying his own life, he only alters the modification of a small portion of matter—only arrests the motion of an animal machine. For, let it be distinctly remembered, that there is no class of men who go so far in denying the real honors, and trampling on the noblest preroga-tives of human nature, as those who are ever prating about the dignity and perfectibility of man. These are the proud teachers, who would persuade us that man is a machine—that the soul is a non-entity—that eternity is a dream—and, of course, that the destruction of life is a trifle unworthy of notice. But woe to the unhappy mortal who, embracing this impious delusion, lifts the murderous hand against his own life! How will he be astonished and con-founded to discover, that the extinction of this mor-tal life is something infinitely more serious than had ever been told him; that it is cutting the "slender thread on which hang everlasting things," that it is terminating the day of grace; that it is putting an end to every opportunity of repentance and refor-mation; that it is hurrying an immortal spirit before the tribunal of its Judge, and fixing the condition of the soul in endless misery, or in endless joy?

But perhaps it will be asked, Can we entertain no hope of the final salvation of one who destroys his own life? This is a question which it ill becomes a blind and erring mortal to decide with confidence. It is possible that a child of God may be so far under the power of mental derangement, as to rush unbidden into the presence of his Father. I believe that instances of this kind have sometimes occurred; and if so, concerning the salvation of such persons no doubt can be entertained. But it may be questioned, on very solid ground, whether a real Christian, in the exercise of his reason, ever became his own executioner. Let those who incline to adopt a more favorable opinion, ponder well that solemn declaration of the Spirit of God, "No murderer hath eternal life abiding in him."[1] How small, then, is the proportion of self-murderers for whom we can cherish the least hope beyond the grave! When men leave the world in an act of daring and deliberate rebellion against God, distrusting his providence, agitated by the worst of passions; and trampling upon all the obligations which bind them to their Creator and their fellow men, how can Charity herself avoid considering them as "strangers to the covenant of promise," and weeping over them as "children of perdition!"

This conclusion will be confirmed, if we look

1  1 John 3:15.

into the sacred history; and examine the characters of Saul, Ahitophel, and Judas, the only instances of suicide which the pen of inspiration has recorded. Do we discover in the last moments of these wretched self-destroyers any thing to warrant a hope concerning their state after death? Alas! no. We find them throughout manifesting that spirit of pride and enmity to God, and that hateful compound of malice and despair, which characterize the fiend, and which torture the bosoms of the accursed in their dark abodes.

With what solemn language, then, does the consideration of his future destiny address every one who contemplates this mode of terminating his earthly sorrows! Pause, O man! and recollect, before the irrevocable step be taken—recollect that thou art to exist beyond the grave! Art thou, then, prepared to die? Art thou sure—miserable as thy present state may be—art thou sure that death will not land thee in still greater misery, in that prison of eternal despair, "where the worm dieth not, and the fire is not quenched,"[1] and where the heaviest calamities of this life will sink into nothing when compared with that "torment, the smoke of which ascendeth for ever and ever?"[2]

Such are the guilt, the folly, and the doom of the self-murderer. May God, of his infinite mercy,

1 Mark 9:44.
2 Revelation 14:11.

preserve us all from an infatuation so deplorable, from a crime of such complicated malignity! "Let me die the death of the righteous, and let my last end be like his!"[1] Amen.

———————

[*Perhaps the following* PAPER *may not improperly conclude this article of the Appendix. It contains a sharp and pointed summary of the arguments against Suicide, and may be considered as a commentary on the sentiments which* COWPER, *at page 42 of the Memoir, has so affectingly recorded, as suggested to his own mind in the hour of temptation, viz.* "THINK WHAT YOU ARE DOING! CONSIDER, AND LIVE!"—]

## DISSUASIVES AGAINST SELF-MURDER

If you are distressed in mind,
*Live;* serenity and joy may yet dawn upon your soul.

If you have been contented and cheerful,
*Live;* and generally diffuse that happiness to others.

If misfortunes have befallen you by your own
     misconduct,
*Live;* and be wiser for the future.

If things have befallen you by the faults of others,
*Live;* you have nothing wherewith to reproach
     yourself.

1 Numbers 23:10.

If you are indigent and helpless,
*Live;* the face of things may agreeably change.

If you are rich and prosperous,
*Live;* and do good with what you possess.

If another hath injured you,
*Live;* his own crime will be his punishment.

If you have injured another,
*Live;* and recompense it by your good offices.

If your character be attacked unjustly,
*Live;* time will remove the aspersion.

If the reproaches are well founded,
*Live;* and deserve them not for the future.

If you are already eminent and applauded,
*Live;* and preserve the honors you have acquired.

If your success is not equal to your merit,
*Live;* in the consciousness of having deserved it.

If your success hath exceeded your merit,
*Live;* and, arrogate not too much to yourself.

If you have been negligent and useless to society,
*Live;* and make amends by your future conduct.

If you have been active and industrious,
*Live;* and communicate your improvement to others.

If you have spiteful enemies,
*Live;* and disappoint their malevolence.

If you have kind and faithful friends,
*Live;* to protect them.

If hitherto you have been impious and wicked,
*Live;* and repent of your sins.

If you have been wise and virtuous,
*Live;* for the future benefit of mankind.

And lastly, If you hope for immortality,
*Live;* and prepare to enjoy it.

## MAN'S QUESTIONS & GOD'S ANSWERS

**Am I accountable to God?**
*Each of us will give an account of himself to God.* ROMANS 14:12 (NIV).

**Has God seen all my ways?**
*Everything is uncovered and laid bare before the eyes of him to whom we must give account.* HEBREWS 4:13 (NIV).

**Does he charge me with sin?**
*But the Scripture declares that the whole world is a prisoner of sin.* GALATIANS 3:22 (NIV).
*All have sinned and fall short of the glory of God.* ROMANS 3:23 (NIV).

**Will he punish sin?**
*The soul who sins is the one who will die.* EZEKIEL 18:4 (NIV).
*For the wages of sin is death, but the gift of God is eternal life in Christ Jesus our Lord.* ROMANS 6:23 (NIV).

**Must I perish?**
*He is patient with you, not wanting anyone to perish, but everyone to come to repentance.* 2 PETER 3:9 (NIV).

**How can I escape?**
*Believe in the Lord Jesus, and you will be saved.* ACTS 16:31 (NIV).

**Is he able to save me?**
*Therefore he is able to save completely those who come to God through him.* HEBREWS 7:25 (NIV).

**Is he willing?**
*Christ Jesus came into the world to save sinners.* 1 TIMOTHY 1:15 (NIV).

**Am I saved on believing?**
*Whoever believes in the Son has eternal life, but whoever rejects the Son will not see life, for God's wrath remains on him.* JOHN 3:36 (NIV).

**Can I be saved now?**
*Now is the time of God's favor, now is the day of salvation.* 2 CORINTHIANS 6:2 (NIV).

**As I am?**
*Whoever comes to me I will never drive away.* JOHN 6:37 (NIV).

**Shall I not fall away?**
*Him who is able to keep you from falling.* JUDE 1:24 (NIV).

**If saved, how should I live?**
*Those who live should no longer live for themselves but for him who died for them and was raised again.* 2 CORINTHIANS 5:15 (NIV).

**What about death and eternity?**
*I am going there to prepare a place for you. I will come back and take you to be with me that you also may be where I am.* JOHN 14:2-3 (NIV).

FOL

AUG 3 ' 2023

Made in the USA
Monee, IL
17 December 2022

22526650R00073